# SOLO
# ON THE YUKON

and

# SOLO ON THE
# YUKON AGAIN

HELEN BROOMELL

SOLO ON THE YUKON
AND OTHER ALASKAN ADVENTURES

BY HELEN BROOMELL

Articles published by *The Lakeland Times* newspaper in 1981,
and in book form by *The Lakeland Times* in 1982.

SOLO ON THE YUKON AGAIN
WITH MORE ALASKAN ADVENTURES

BY HELEN BROOMELL

Articles published by *The Lakeland Times* newspaper in 1983,
and in book form by Helen Broomell in 1984.

SOLO ON THE YUKON AND
SOLO ON THE YUKON AGAIN

BY HELEN BROOMELL

Republished with copyright license from *The Lakeland Times.*

Published by LinguaConcepts, Alexandria, NH

ISBN 978-1-300-83157-0

# PREFACE TO THE REPUBLISHED VERSION

HELEN BROOMELL HAD LIVED IN MINOCQUA, WISCONSIN FOR THIRTY-THREE years when she went on her first Alaskan adventure. She had been the director of Camp Minocqua, first with her husband Jack and later with her son Dare, and was well known for her friendliness and wide-ranging interests. After her first two trips to Alaska, when she paddled approximately 1,350 miles of the Yukon River by herself, she became known throughout Wisconsin through articles in newspapers and magazines, radio and television interviews, and talks she gave to groups all over the state.

Helen sent back articles from both her Yukon River trips, which were published at the time by *The Lakeland Times*. The articles were preserved for posterity by their publication in book form *(Solo on the Yukon*, published by *The Lakeland Times,* and *Solo on the Yukon Again,* published by Helen herself). The books enabled relatives, friends, and canoe adventurers to relive her experiences and remember her good nature, warmth, and kindness.

In the intervening years, Helen's books have gone out of print, and used copies are difficult to find. Several years ago, one of Helen's oldest friends suggested I explore ways to make the books available again. Writing and self-publishing a book about Helen's life *(A Helluva Life: As lived by Helen Sprague Broomell)* showed me that I could deal with the complexities required to republish the *Solo* books: editing, formatting, and scanning and adjusting photographs, and *The Lakeland Times* graciously gave me a copyright license agreement to do so. I made as few changes as possible to the original versions: the type is a little larger, and the quality of many of the photographs has been improved. I made only those changes to the text that were necessary for clarity and correctness.

My motivation to republish these books is the same as Don Walker's, publisher of *The Lakeland Times,* as stated in his Preface to the first *Solo* book: to inspire others to adventures of their own.

*Sue Broomell Irujo*

*Editor and publisher*

# SOLO
# ON THE YUKON

and other Alaskan Adventures

*By Helen Broomell*

# TABLE OF CONTENTS I

# PREFACE

THIS ACCOUNT OF ONE PERSON'S ADVENTURES IN THE FAR NORTH CAME TO US in weekly installments, more or less, during a five-month period in 1981, and was published in *The Lakeland Times.*

Helen Broomell, grandmother of ten, who was 65 years old at the time, fulfilled a lifelong ambition to canoe one of the big rivers of the country by paddling solo some 600 miles down the Yukon River in Alaska. This was only the start of her adventures, which culminated in a dogsledding trip with friends in November.

Her future plans include a return trip to Alaska to paddle another six or eight hundred miles further down the Yukon, visit her friends, and spend some time in the southeast part of the state.

Because so many people requested copies of the articles, *The Lakeland Times* has published this book. The pictures are from Helen's own slides. We hope you may be inspired to adventures of your own.

*Don Walker*

*Publisher, The Lakeland Times*

# INTRODUCTION

*"The Great Land," showing routes covered by car, plane, train,
Alaska Ferry, hitchhiking, and any other available means.*

WITHIN EACH OF US THERE MUST BE, AT LEAST OCCASIONALLY, A DESIRE TO
simplify our life and at the same time reach out to new and challenging
experiences. To some that could mean dumping the "rat race" and
moving to a community where the pace is slower, or perhaps, in the
spirit of our early settlers, it could be a try for a life in the wilderness or
on a small farm. To others it might mean an ocean cruise or an
extensive vacation trip to a faraway place.

But whatever challenge one chooses, the experience could be only a shallow one if it's not combined with an expanding of the horizons of the mind as well. What good is it to travel afar and never get to know the people and their customs? We need to open our minds to make room for many different levels of knowledge and ways of seeing the world around us.

This is what I've tried to do during my five months of travel in Alaska. I have learned much from the Eskimo and the Indian, and have gained a deeper insight into my own nature. My appreciation goes to all the new friends who now have become old friends, whose warmth and help along the way made it all work. The entire trip flowed from one experience to another with much the same positive manner as the mighty Yukon, and with about as many meanderings as I encountered paddling through the Yukon Flats!

Why Alaska? It goes back forty years, to be specific, originating with a man who is now something of a legend in Alaska; an old sourdough (old timer) by the name of Slim Williams. He died not too many years ago in Chicago, only a few years short of celebrating his hundredth birthday; and his widow, Gladys, lives in her home state of Indiana.

Slim's story goes back many years to the time of the Klondike Gold Rush of 1897. With neither family nor home, he joined the thousands heading north to search for gold in the already-famous Dawson area. The difference was that Slim, at age 15, had no interest in the gold, but was attracted to Alaska from his home in California purely for the adventure of it. That he had, and eventually he collaborated with Richard Morenus to write his autobiography, *Alaska Sourdough.*

He came into my life in 1941, when he decided to look up the "best boy's camp" (he said) in the United States, in order to find skilled teenage campers who might be interested in joining a small group to travel Alaska's woods and waters with him. When he met my father, Dr. Sprague, and learned about Camp Minocqua, he knew he had the right place, and with travel restrictions enforced during World War II, he had to postpone his travels, so remained with us four summers. He set up our outpost camp, taught the boys and staff log cabin building, and told stories about Alaska that had the boys sitting on the edge of their chairs in suspense and excitement.

*Slim Williams, who inspired my interest in Alaska, shown in front of one of the cabins he built with Camp Minocqua campers in 1942.*

Slim ran sled-dog mail routes after the big gold stampedes, and was best known for his success in crossbreeding Alaskan huskies and wolves. He eventually drove a team from Skagway, Alaska to Chicago to represent Alaska at the 1933 World's Fair. It took many pairs of handmade booties for the dogs and wheels for the sled when they got out of snow country. He not only made it successfully, but went on to Washington, D.C. to tell the politicians what route he thought the proposed Alaska-Canada Highway should go.

*On his first trip "Outisde" since arriving in Alaska in 1897, Slim Williams stopped over in Chicago for the World's Fair, and then went on to Washington, D.C. to lobby for the Alaska Highway.*

There was a move a few years ago, pushed by Yukon Territory pioneer Laurent Cyr, to rename the Cassiar Highway Slim Williams Way, but it didn't make it through the political tangles of Provincial government.

Because of so many years spent in the Bush (Slim didn't own a pair of store-bought shoes from age 15 to age 50!), it's no wonder that his life and stories were a strong influence on my desire to go to

Alaska. And although Slim would scarcely recognize parts of the country now, there are still thousands of miles of unbounded wilderness and a true frontier lifestyle in a good part of the state.

Preparation for the trip was spread over a length of time. It needn't have taken so long, but the enjoyment involved made it worthwhile. After reading everything I could find about the state, its history, geography, economy, and current status, I bought maps and studied them carefully. And, of course, a large amount of "tourist information" needed to be read and sorted out.

Assembling items to take involved many decisions. The first part of the trip, which was on the river, posed no problem, as I could take whatever I needed, but everything necessary after that was carefully weighed, ounce by ounce, to minimize the weight of the backpack. The usual tendency is to take too much—I did, and as a result, sent more boxes home than would have been necessary.

By the time I had traveled a month or so out of a backpack, there was one change of clothing and only absolute essentials in it, which cut down the weight to around forty pounds, and made it possible for me to carry a book or two, or a few gifts. Absolute essentials: good rain gear, including rubber boots; a comfortable sleeping system; and most important, an open mind and a positive attitude.

The final plans for this Great Alaskan Adventure came together like a completed jigsaw puzzle, and after 10 days of leisurely traveling, I was glad to be (while still in Yukon Territory) the first "foreign correspondent" for the *Lakeland Times*.

# CHAPTER 1

# Down the River with Paddle and Pack

GETTING THE CANOE TO DAWSON SEEMED AN ALMOST INSURMOUNTABLE problem, as I didn't want to bring my car, but "a friend of a friend" came to the rescue. Ed Berg of Madison was planning on driving to Alaska with a friend, his daughter, and a friend of hers, so we have been a congenial group of five on the road, comfortably squeezed into a large van. Ed customized the interior to provide a sleeping deck for two, which is made up of many 8-inch-deep compartments with lift-up lids for storing carpenter tools, books, and all kinds of supplies. Underneath the deck are three wooden boxes for food, kitchen things, and the remaining space for personal gear. Convenient.

*The van is loaded and we're ready to take off.*

We have two tents, although mine is as yet unused, as I prefer a bivvy sack arrangement, which is a waterproof breathable cover for a sleeping bag, complete with head cover and mosquito netting. Ideal for traveling, but there will be times when a tent is necessary.

We have camped in Provincial or National parks in Canada, and in town parks or with friends in the States.

Some highlights of the journey, beginning in Wisconsin: a visit to the Whaleback Ship Museum in Superior; to the Iron Range Interpretative Center in Chisholm, Minnesota, which is a new museum of mining, funded by the taconite tax, that is both beautiful and informative; a stay with the young people working at the Delta Waterfront Research Center in Manitoba, which operates under the auspices of the National Wildlife Federation; ducks everywhere, many yellow-headed blackbirds, and dozens of varieties of other birds; the typical onion-shaped domed churches of Manitoba's Ukrainian Orthodox churches; a delicate, low-arched rainbow against dark grey threatening skies with the sun shining on one of Alberta's great wheat fields; a surprise dinner out (I should say "in") at an excellent Chinese restaurant in Edmonton; the gradual change from large farm to small farm to small ranch, to the mountainous area of the northern Rocky Mountains of Alberta and British Columbia; and finally, at Dawson Creek, the beginning of the 1,200 mile long Alaska Highway.

Built by the U.S. Army Corps of Engineers in only eight months, and completed in 1942 to provide a land route for supplies to Alaska during the war, the highway is an experience in itself. While much of it is paved, it varies from excellent to very poor, with chuck holes, mud, rock slides, and road equipment to keep a driver alert. There are breathtaking views of heavily forested mountains, swift rivers, and quiet lakes surrounded by the ever-present northern spruce.

Traffic seems heavy. We have seen hundreds of motor homes and campers, singly and in groups, old buses, dilapidated cars, and even bicycles, all heading north for their own great adventure, carrying bikes, boats, dog houses, pets, kids, and old folks. Also a few young people with all of their belongings stuffed inside, and attached somewhat precariously to the outside, of their vehicles, who obviously plan to remain and settle in the North.

A stop on the Alaska Highway in British Columbia that few people miss is the Provincial Park at the Liard River, where there is a fine hot spring for bathing. The water temperature is 120 degrees and constantly flowing. Very warm, but one becomes accustomed to it,

*Typical view along the Alaska Highway,*
*but the road wasn't always this smooth!*

and the euphoric feeling of floating in such beautiful surroundings is never to be forgotten, especially after long hours of driving.

It's interesting that at this time of year, it's possible to read a book at midnight with no artificial light. How strange it must be to go further north and watch the sun travel around the horizon!

Whitehorse is the capital of Yukon Territory, and is located on the upper Yukon River. The population of 16,000 is two thirds of the total in the province, so there's not much competition for space, especially when one realizes that all of the New England states (or England) would fit inside its borders!

The decision not to start the canoe trip in Whitehorse was based on my desire to avoid the tourist boats and general confusion of the city.

Weather? Couldn't be more beautiful. Quite different from Wisconsin, as this is an arid climate, and although there are almost constant dark clouds in one direction or another, and occasional brief showers, the mountains catch most of the rain and the sun shines all day. There is no dew, which is a convenience when sleeping out.

In Dawson the Summer Solstice (longest day of the year) is celebrated by most of the population hiking to the top of Midnight Dome, just outside the city, to watch the sun at 12 midnight— accompanied, of course, by much singing and revelry.

Because of the long days of sunshine, plants grow extraordinarily large, and the roadsides and river banks are covered with purple, blue, and yellow flowers. The wild rose predominates, and there are hundreds of blossoms within a few feet of where we camped.

Dawson City is in the throes of transforming itself from a ghost town of the old Klondike gold-rush days to a thriving tourist community, and it's a difficult process. The Canadian government has restored the old opera house, where we saw *The Follies,* a musical production of the history of the town during the years following the discovery of gold by George Carmacks in 1896. It was a fine, professional production.

The audience was a strange mix of tour-bus people, travel-camper people, backpackers and canoeists, local tourist-oriented citizens, and the hard-core miners, explorers, and supply people who cover the North with their helicopters and equipment.

Other buildings are also restored, but most are barely standing after all these years. It's a dusty, mixed-up, new-old town.

The river here is about a quarter of a mile wide, with a current of six or seven miles an hour, which is just fine, and explains why excursions on the river are called float trips. As the river widens (at one point it is 10 miles wide, with many islands), the current decreases, of course.

The mountains are out of sight from here, but there are cliffs along the river and high hills in all directions. We camped in a grove of cottonwood trees, across the river by free ferry from the town, and for general traffic this is pretty much the end of the line.

It was a sunny Saturday afternoon on June 27 when I launched the canoe in Dawson, Yukon Territory, and after only five days of paddling arrived in Eagle, Alaska. By measuring with a flexible plant stem along the river's route on the Canadian and U.S. topographic maps, it comes to 110 miles. That's an average of 28 miles a day, with no difficulty except a strong head wind one day, which brought white caps with it. Best not to "float" under those circumstances.

The Yukon River has long served as a pathway of migration and travel. During Gold Rush days, stampeders, enduring unbelievable hardships, swarmed down the Yukon from its headwaters in a multitude of jerrybuilt crafts, and up the river from its mouth in paddlewheel steamboats, to the gold fields of the Klondike, the Fortymile, and other rivers. Throughout the 1880s and 1890s, the Yukon was the Mississippi of the North, serving as the transportation route for hordes of prospectors and for tons of supplies. Now, moldering cabins and abandoned equipment remain to recall that era. But before all that, and through the years, it has been the home of the Han and Kutchin Tribes of the Athabascan Indians.

The Yukon is one of the great rivers of the world. It drains an area of 330,000 square miles (one third of Alaska), and is 2,300 miles long. It carries the glacial silt from thousands of icy peaks, which accounts for its milky appearance and the strange, very soft tinkling sound one hears when traveling in an aluminum canoe.

The country is magnificent, and more beautiful, of course, when seen from the river. It is bordered by high cliffs on one side or another, which are remarkably able to sustain spindly spruce trees in the cracks of the rock. Willow and poplar grow profusely, but nothing grows very tall except in the flatter areas. The sky is always interesting, except on completely overcast days, as there are frequent storm cloud formations over the mountains, with bright sunshine combined.

Lacking a geologist's or rock hound's background, I can't say much about the rock formations except that there is a great variety. There is granite, shale, a lot of greenstone, and huge pieces of pure quartz, along with many large boulders worn smooth from their travels downriver.

The shores, particularly the outside curves, show the effects of the damage done at breakup time, when blocks of ice weighing tons come crashing downstream, demolishing anything in their way. Bark is stripped from trees 30 feet above the river, and large boulders are shoved along the shore, while entire trees of all sizes are carried away, some to go as far as the ocean. There the Yupik Eskimos live in a land barren of trees, but with a seemingly endless supply of timber.

The wildlife is here, although to date I've seen small animals and birds of all kinds, but only tracks of bear, moose, and a wolf. On one of the mucky beach areas near a stream where I stopped for lunch, it looked from the tracks as though the wolf had unsuccessfully chased a moose into the deep muck and out again.

To be on the river is to be in a world apart. The feeling of complete isolation, with no sight or sound of another human for many days, is to me something to cherish and enjoy to the fullest.

One such pleasure is the variety of sounds heard from the river. One is the tinkling of the tiny rivulets coming down from the mountains, and magnified in volume many times over by the chasm from which they emerge. And when the current meets an obstruction or rushes against the rock, it sounds as if it were a small rapids.

Most surprising was a sound I heard once but may never hear again. It was a thunderous, muffled noise that resembled dynamite in the distance, but I could actually feel the reverberations. After about 30 seconds a large wave appeared close to me, accompanied by back eddies and whitewater breaking in one spot. It was a very large underwater boulder that had been moved by the great power of the river into a position closer to the surface, though probably still many feet underwater.

The first night out I made camp on one of the many small islands which extend into gravel bars. It cools down at night to 35 or 40 degrees, but is in the 60s or 70s during the day. It's easy to keep warm in my down sleeping bag inside a bivvy sack, and the mosquitoes aren't bad—yet! So I haven't bothered to put up a tent.

Dinner one night was rice and dried vegetables in a tomato sauce. Lunches are cold, snack-type meals with crackers, dried fruits, nuts, jerky (homemade), and granola, along with lemonade.

*Typical campsite along the river. The five-cup pot holds all my cooking needs, including a small stove when it's not in use.*

The second night there was no island close by, so I climbed a high bank and nestled in under the pines on a bed of sphagnum moss (dry), being careful not to occupy a game trail. It's wise to cook a distance from where one sleeps, and a must to either hang food from a high branch out of reach of the bears, or have it so thoroughly wrapped and packaged that no odor escapes. I chose the latter method and trust it will be effective. Someone told me that Alaska is cat-and-mouse country—just be sure you remember who is the mouse. Well said.

The third night I reached the abandoned town of Fortymile, so named because it was 40 miles from Fort Egbert. It existed for only a few years during the gold rush, with a store, a few cabins, a Royal Northwest Mounted Police post, and an Anglican church, all still in good repair, although everyone left in 1898. The Yukon Province plans to restore it. I slept in the shadow of the church and felt unusually safe.

The next day brought me to the U.S.-Canadian border, where I camped close by a beautiful stream. Met two Germans who spoke no English, but who managed to let me know that they were planning to travel the entire length of the river—with a motor. Supplemented my dinner with a large helping of lamb's quarter—that great edible weed that grows wild almost everywhere.

Day four brings me to Eagle, Alaska, the town so well written about by John McPhee in his book *Coming into the Country*. It's about the friendliest town I've ever visited, and has a pleasant, relaxed atmosphere. It is connected to the outside world by a road (summer only), and there are a few tourists in every day, but people who live here tend to stay put.

Conversations in the post office with some of the townspeople involved plans for a Fourth of July celebration, the next town meeting, how to tan bear and lynx hides, and a complaint from one that his taxes had increased 100 per cent in the past year, from six dollars to twelve dollars!

The Eagle postmaster, John Borg, grew up in Spirit, Wisconsin, near Tomahawk, but has been in Alaska since World War II and in Eagle for a number of years. He is acquainted with Gladys and Carl Bauers of Woodruff, Wisconsin and Glenallen, Alaska. By the time I had strolled the quarter mile of main street, mistaken the general store for a restaurant, asked for a cup of coffee, received it, and discovered my mistake when I couldn't pay for it, I felt that this had to be one of the friendliest towns in the country.

And by the next day, after I had spent the night camped on a hill overlooking the river, I had three invitations to be the guest of 1) two charming girls who are living in a teepee just outside of town, 2) an elderly gentleman who is a CB freak, and 3) the two girls and their four boys who own the general store. I chose the latter, and was almost forcefully invited to remain another couple of days—for a steak dinner and a salmon feast the next evening.

This is a log cabin town, with a central water supply originally

*The old well house in Eagle, built at the turn of the century,
and still supplying most of the water for the town.*

operated by a windmill built in 1898, and still supplying almost all the water needed.

Historically, Eagle is an interesting settlement. It was the first incorporated town in the interior of Alaska, and was the site of Fort Egbert, which is now being partially restored by the Bureau of Land Management. It has been interesting visiting with the people I have read about in McPhee's book, and I plan to keep in touch with these new friends.

The mornings are overcast, but the haze is from the forest fires outside of Fairbanks. Crews are being sent from all the villages, as there are over 20 fires in the state. In spite of the drizzle, and after my first washtub bath and shampoo in a long time, I said goodbye to Eagle.

For about a hundred miles after entering Alaska, the river flows through the Yukon-Charlie National Forest. These lands are a part of the almost 800 million acres acquired by the Federal Government when President Carter signed the Alaska Lands Bill just before leaving office. In this area, the exposed rock formations are unique in all of the country, and date back to Precambrian times. Although I saw no fossils, I spotted a falcon's nest high on a craggy cliff. Whether a gyrfalcon or a peregrine was a question. Arctic grayling and salmon are plentiful, and in this National Forest the tributaries of the Yukon are closed to salmon fishing. As I traveled north, the lovely Arctic tern joined me. Truly the most beautiful and graceful bird I have ever seen, and a most-accomplished aerial gymnast!

During the more leisurely stretches of the river it has been interesting to think that I am seeing the same river and the same country, with very few differences, that the prehistoric Indian saw— or the early explorer, or the Hudson's Bay trader, or the Klondike stampeder, or the sled-running mailman. There are fewer visible reminders of them than I would have imagined.

The Yukon flows free, and with the exception of one dam fairly close to its source, there are no man-made obstructions in its way to the ocean. The changes result from the course of the river going from northwest to southwest, from the mountainous area to the interior, which is appropriately called the Yukon Flats. Now the river widens, forming many channels (called braiding), sometimes covering as much as ten miles in width. Choosing a course is often a problem, as I proved by missing the town of Circle completely. Rain and high winds combined to conceal the village until it was too late to get to shore across the current. The decision to go ashore must be made about a quarter of a mile ahead of time, and there is no possibility of canoeing upstream! I was sorry to miss Circle, as it was known during its brief heyday (1890–1899) as "The Paris of the North." Thousands of stampeders enjoyed the opera house and library, as well as the dance halls and saloons.

While I was in Eagle, the first of the salmon arrived on their way upriver to spawn, and many fishermen were preparing to set nets. The only ones I saw during the week between Eagle and Fort Yukon were two Natives on their way to their fishing grounds, but as I got closer to this village, there were four or five large fish wheels in operation. The river current operates this basket-type, revolving affair that automatically dumps the fish into a large underwater box after being caught in the wheel. A very ancient (and efficient) method. The gill nets are more of a problem, as they collect debris from the river.

Several nights this past week were spent on gravel bars, and with a change in the weather from light rains and mostly sun to rain steadily for almost three days, I was glad to have a good tent along. One night an old prospector's cabin furnished a roof over my head, while I slept on the six-foot-long table—the only flat place inside. The tin roof flapped all night and the thoughts of former occupants filled my mind while I wasn't sleeping.

The following day I was greeted by two moose. One, a cow, fairly close, browsing along the edge of a slough, and the other a good-sized bull across the river. Good to have binoculars so I could watch them feed. As if that wasn't enough, sometime late in the day a black bear emerged from the alder bushes and slowly ambled along the shore for about a quarter of a mile, paying no attention to my presence a hundred yards away.

Because I have always felt a closeness to our north country loons, and never ceased to marvel at them, I've been looking forward to seeing the northern red loon. Yesterday one flew over, crying its lonesome call, but sounding slightly different than its southern cousins, so I'm hoping to see one at closer range.

As I neared Fort Yukon, it was essential to do some careful navigating—I couldn't afford to miss another village. The islands are

*Excellent shelter. Just over five pounds complete,*
*and big enough for two people to sit up in.*

confusing, but by correctly figuring the current, I came out suddenly facing what at first seemed to be two fifty-story skyscrapers, combined with some other building. Nothing on the maps to indicate this, and it seemed I had been transported to some science fiction setting, but as I paddled on, the village of Fort Yukon was a welcome sight. After all the rain and wind, I was ready to go ashore. Later, I found that the strange sight I had seen was the Early Warning System (Dew Line) of the Armed Services, which is manned by about 35 Air Force staff.

After a muddy half mile to "downtown" Fort Yukon and back to the apparently falling-down Sourdough Inn, only to find they had no room available, I met two young men who suggested that my canoe and belongings weren't safe from theft merely pulled up on shore. They carried all my gear, one offered his sofa (Kris Krestensen, the Social Services officer), while the other (Bill Black, elementary school teacher), who lives next door, whipped up a delicious caribou rib dinner. What a break for me! I hadn't been chilled on the river, but did discover that I was pretty wet.

Fort Yukon is the air hub of northern interior Alaska, and is located at the confluence of the Porcupine River and the Yukon. It was founded as a Hudson's Bay trading post in 1847, and is the largest Native village on the Yukon, as well as the oldest English-speaking settlement in the state. It's a surprise to find about fifty cars in a town with only eight miles of roads! Gwitchin is the native language of these Kutchin Athabascans, and there is a couple living here that is teaching it, and, in their spare time, translating the Bible into Gwitchin.

Water is a problem, as the permafrost is only a few feet down. Yukon River water is piped through a treatment system and is delivered either by truck (for a fee), or by hand, to the cabins from a central source. Some of the log cabins still have sod roofs, but the majority are covered with the shining tin roof typical of the North. The community is cluttered; muddy when wet and dusty when dry, and almost all the buildings are log. There are three churches—the Episcopal (Anglican) Church being famous for its white moose-hide, beaded altar cloth, which is exquisite in detail and workmanship. There is a fine small museum here, which I enjoyed, and in both Eagle and Fort Yukon I have been fortunate to be able to visit with Native artists who are doing various crafts.

I've been lucky to be included in local activities, and one highlight of this visit was a trip by outboard about three miles upriver to check Bill Black's fishnet. It was pretty well messed up with sticks and logs, so it took a long time to get it off the bottom. At one point, Kris gave a hard tug, the net came loose, and he toppled over backwards into the water. It's only about 40 degrees, so it was a quick dip in and out, and then a big driftwood fire to ward off hypothermia. There was a 40-pound king salmon and a sheefish in the net—a good haul. What a delicacy fresh salmon is!

The Fourth of July was interesting, with afternoon games for the children—the same as almost everywhere. Rather than join the public dance in the evening, Kris and I were invited to join four young people who are part of a Campfire, Inc. group whose aim is to bring a simple recreational and water safety program to the Native children in outlying villages of Alaska. Much needed. As a retired camp director, it was interesting for me to hear of their problems and talk about the program. We were indebted to them for turning out a fresh-caught baked salmon, salad, and quiche dinner in true gourmet style. Then some good conversation and enough time and a good location for watching the sunset and sunrise all at one time for an hour or so as the orange-flowing sun moved around the horizon without falling out of sight. I was too tired to watch after 1:00 a.m., so I went to bed, but it's still strange to have daylight for 24 hours and see children out playing in the middle of the night.

Speaking of food, here are some current prices: bread $2 a loaf, eggs $2.10 a dozen, a can of chili and beans $3.50, so it's no wonder that a meal out here runs at least $15. Kris got a special on 2x4x8s for some remodeling, and they were $4.50 each. Gasoline is $2.74 per gallon, and everything in the village either comes in by barge or by plane, which explains the cost. It also explains why people here are subsistence hunters, fishermen, and trappers. We said goodbye to a young man who is leaving for his trapline 200 miles northeast of here on the Porcupine River. He will go by boat and a plane will carry his supplies up for $800—transportation only. His next trip to town will be in about nine months.

Back on the river again, with many interesting changes in its character. As a result of the junction with the Porcupine River, there is even more debris floating down. All sizes and shapes of trees, logs, and branches slide by. Because of recent rains, the water level is high, and more and more mud banks are kerplopping into the current, along with whatever had been growing on the bank. I watched a 30-foot spruce slowly topple in and be carried away, complete with moss and ferns growing among its roots.

These trees travel at a great rate in the current, and several times

*Hitching a ride with a friendly tree.*

I've hitched a ride for many miles with a friendly tree. Mostly now I'm seeing smaller logs and branches, frequently resembling sea serpents, dragons, and the like. Fun to watch.

With only a few more days to go on the river, a little backtracking would be a good idea. In these weeks my paddling experiences have gone from one extreme to the other: from carefree floating to really working. (That reminds me of another good new book on Alaska, called *Going to Extremes,* by Joe McGinnis. Controversial up here.)

Weather continues to be erratic, with occasional sun and a lot of overcast and wind. The first night out of Fort Yukon there was serious doubt in my mind whether the tent would stand the almost gale-force winds, and I vowed never again to make camp on a gravel bar, no matter how bright and sunny the weather when I pull in. The winds kept me ashore for a layover day, much appreciated after the noise and commotion of the Fourth of July in town.

Now that the river has spread into the Yukon Flats, navigation is a problem. Not really a problem, as the current will always take me downstream, but some choices involve an extra 50 miles of travel, or an advantage in getting out of the wind, or any number of decisions that make it hard for me to say, "I'll just float it." I was temporarily misplaced for almost three days, and when I figured out where I was I had just slept on Deadman's Island.

The Flats aren't as marshy as I expected, and there is land high enough to camp on. And yes, there are mosquitoes by the millions, but I have to plug L.L. Bean's Shoo Bug net jacket impregnated with repellent, because it really keeps them away.

And yes, I have sore and tired muscles from trying to cross the

*Air view (taken later in the trip) of the "braided" river in the Yukon Flats area, downriver from Fort Yukon.*

current, particularly after a time when the river narrowed, the flow speed picked up, and the wind did, too. I had no choice but to ride out the stretch of two-foot waves. It was exhilarating, to put it mildly.

At one time I rounded a bend and was immediately besieged by about 50 frantic, screaming, diving gulls. My first thought was that they wanted fish scraps, but there is so little traffic on that part of the river that I ruled it out. Then I noticed a bobbing group of fuzzy little birds that I thought were ducks, but which turned out to be baby gulls that couldn't yet fly. There must have been 30 or more. I thought I was going to be dive-bombed before I got away.

Later a squadron of ducks flew by just six inches above the water in perfect formation. One more moose seen across the river, more Arctic loons, and many varieties of birds unfamiliar to me.

I stopped in the Athabascan village of Beaver for fresh water, as there are no clear streams in the Yukon Flats, and Artie Adams, the postmaster, was eager to have me meet his mother, Charlotte. So we enjoyed an hour or so of good talk and good coffee. At 75, she leads an active life, after raising 10 children alone following the death of her husband. She says, "No hunger here. Hunger everywhere, but no hunger at my house in old days." Her typical singsong manner of speech was so lilting and lovely that I could have stayed to listen for hours more. Her early memories of the "old way" of living were vivid, and she told stories about the steamboats and the river people, as well as about their hunting and fishing camps.

There are changes going on everywhere, but nowhere is it more noticeable then in the Indian villages. The clash of cultures brings problems, and alcoholism is the greatest one; but on the bright side, the old languages are being taught, old skills are being revived, and the old cultures may be saved. With ample state funds, there is no dearth of programs and funds available to the villages, and constant improvements are being made.

Each village now has a treated water supply and a community building with showers and hot water. Airport improvement is underway in Beaver, and they seem to be making a road, although there isn't a car or truck in town!

The town is only a cluster of cabins around the general store/post office that appears not to have changed in the past 50 years. The typical trademark of the northern communities, whether Indian or Eskimo, is the blue oil barrel, usually piled up on the waterfront along with all the other used-up or broken-down equipment. Things don't get repaired, they get replaced, and there is no way of disposing of anything underground because of the permafrost. I watched in amazement as a long barge went by, loaded with heavy equipment and hundreds of gallons of oil, and wondered how it navigated the many turns in the river.

Snowmobiles have become an integral part of life in the North, but there are many who either prefer to travel by snowshoe and dog team, or enjoy the sport of racing a team. Consequently, every village has its many dogs, who spend all of their time chained when not being worked. Just as well, as they're not always friendly creatures. Avid racers (and some who take tourists out) put their sleds on wheels and run the teams during the summer, but mostly they stay tied up. Howling (sometimes called singing), is their chief occupation, and 20 or 30 animals can get quite a concert going. I'm amazed at the different sounds they make, but then, some may be part wolf.

Two more canoeists turned up outside of Beaver. One, a carpenter who had built a cabin I visited in Eagle, the other a painter at Prudhoe Bay, on their way back to Fairbanks. They travel faster, so went on, but I shared a wild rice, onion, and beef (jerky) stew with them. (The wild rice I cooked at home, then dried in the warming oven of my range, and presto!—instant wild rice.)

The last two days on the river brought me out of the Yukon Flats and into faster-moving water and more mountainous terrain.

The river narrowed to only one channel again, and it was a relief not to have to follow the map so carefully. Rain off and on every day, but none of it the drenching Wisconsin type.

More fish wheels in operation, but because of the high water many people are having trouble keeping them working properly. Passed quite a few boats tending to their nets or wheels, as well as many more fish camps, where the Indians set up a temporary camp while they dry and/or smoke their fish. The aroma often caught me many miles before I reached them.

The search for drinking water brought me to a small creek running down from the mountain. It proved to be the site of an old army fort, according to the map, though there was no visible sign of it, and the area was completely overgrown. It was a beautiful campsite.

Sometime during the night I heard ominous rumblings and thrashing in the underbrush near my tent, but by the time I unzipped the tent there was nothing to be seen.

The following day brought me to the end of my river journey, and with it a real regret at having to leave it. The ever-changing Yukon and I have become good friends, although I'll have to confess that after three weeks there are still many aspects of her personality that remain a riddle to me.

However, if nothing else, she has imprinted me with a great respect for her moods and her caprices. Docile and euphoric at one minute, she can assume an entirely opposite role in a few brief moments, and in partnership with the wind, can become angry and turbulent almost beyond belief. Rather like temper tantrums, as they rarely last for any length of time.

Perhaps sometime I'll return.

# CHAPTER 2

# Education
# and
# Native Games

IT WAS HARD TO SAY GOODBYE TO MY FAITHFUL LITTLE CANOE, BUT IT WILL BE IN good hands and happy to remain on the river. I figure we covered approximately 600 miles, from Dawson City, Yukon Territory, to the bridge at the haul road.

This road was built during the construction of the pipeline, and goes from the port of Valdez on the Gulf of Alaska, on the south, to Prudhoe Bay on the Arctic Ocean, on the north. It has been open to the public up to the bridge for several years, and has now been opened for another 175 or so miles further north. The only available services are at the bridge, and the road in some places makes the Alaska Highway seem like a boulevard, so traffic is discouraged.

An enterprising young man named Ken Menzies owns the truck stop at the bridge, and after looking over the two odd hovercrafts that were used to ferry pipeline supplies across the river before the bridge was built, I asked him if I could leave my canoe for him to sell. No problem, but I later changed my mind and asked him to store it for me so I could resume my trip in another year.

So the next project was to find a ride into Fairbanks (110 miles) for me and my assorted gear. Some things are to be sent home, some things left in Fairbanks to be used later (trail food), and everything else consolidated to go into my backpack. Most cars driven by tourists were already overloaded, but eventually a man who works for the highway department came in driving a new pickup, and I was off in a cloud of dust—quite literally.

Views from the highway were spectacular, as it wound around and over the hills and small mountains, often within sight of the never-ending silver worm of a pipeline, also winding its way along the same route. The pipeline is constructed to keep the permafrost from melting, and is well insulated whether above or below ground.

Arrival at a shopping mall in Fairbanks was a real shocker. The noise and confusion and traffic and people combined to make me feel quite disoriented, but after a taxi ride to a local campground I began to recover.

There are advantages to being a member of the American Youth Hostel (no age limit; my 65 years don't preclude membership), as the camping fee is only $2 instead of $7.50 for a night.

Not much sleep the first night, though, as the airport was next to the campground. Too much contrast between that and the absolute silence of the nights on the river. It was a treat to have a hot shower and a laundry. The other section of the campground is full of trucks and RVs from all over the country.

So now a different part of my trip begins.

Fairbanks is an interesting city, second largest in the state, with a population of about 25,000. Founded in the early 1900s when gold was discovered in the area, it is a combination of bits of old Alaska and the new. There are still log cabin homes within the city limits, beautifully cared for, and with large vegetable gardens and flowers galore.

In other parts of the city, it looks very much like any other middle-sized city in any other part of the country, with its four-lane bypass and new shopping malls.

What sets it apart is the character of the people who live here, and their attitudes toward one another and toward their state and its problems. Alaska has always attracted independent people who don't like to be told what to do, and who will do anything to help another in times of trouble. A good example of this was during a flood a few years ago. Everyone with boats, tents, and survival equipment quietly went about their way rescuing people whose homes were underwater, releasing dogs that were tied, and in general taking care of the situation, while the city's Civil Defense organization was still trying to get itself organized.

The next few days I spent sightseeing and getting my land legs back again. There is much history in the area, and the confluence of the Chena and Tanana Rivers (which flow into the Yukon) was a logical spot for a town after the discovery of gold in the area. There are excellent museums and libraries here, as well as the University of Alaska, which provides further facilities and opportunities to the Fairbanksians.

There are interesting goings and comings at the Youth Hostel campground. Many foreign young people from Germany, Sweden, and Japan, as well as the U.S., are here now. Most speak excellent English, and we've had good conversations. But after a few days, Celia Hunter, with whom I had some correspondence earlier, invited me to stay with her and her friend Ginny Wood. It has been a rare privilege. They live about eight miles out of town in a typically Alaskan log cabin, with their two Husky dogs. They both ferried planes for the Air Force in Alaska during World War II, and following that took a job with Arctic Air Tours (which later became Westours). In 1950 they founded Camp Denali, a rustic resort just outside McKinley Park.

After 25 years of operation, Celia and Ginny retired, Celia to become for a time the president of the Wilderness Society, and to devote more time to writing on environmental subjects. Ginny is leading backpacking trips, most recently in the Arctic Wildlife Range on the North Slope.

*From the left, Celia Hunter, me, and Ginny Wood.*

My activities at their house included helping to package and freeze 75 pounds of silver salmon, which was purchased from an Indian on the river for 50 cents a pound; digging post holes for a support for their woodpile; and weeding a very large vegetable garden. Things grow to tremendous size here because of the long days.

One day we visited all the neighbors in Dogpatch, which is the name of their area. One is a young Austrian family with a lovely home filled with stained glass, greenery, and a beautiful enameled wood stove. Another couple is a potter and photographer who have three sons who are artists—like walking into a museum! And still another is a fine carpenter, in the process of building a large solar-heated home for his family.

Although I prefer to be camping rather than in town, there were good reasons for my staying over. One was a week-long comprehensive course at the University of Alaska, titled Workshop on Alaska. The subjects covered included geography; history; climate; birds; mammals; plants and vegetation; geology; mining; agriculture; Native affairs, artifacts, and languages; education; energy resources; and a final session on Alaska's future. This was presented by Robert Weeden, whose book *Alaska, Promises to Keep* was the first book I read on present-day Alaska, and I would recommend it highly to anyone interested in the state.

One highlight of the course was a field trip to the Silver Fox mine—a silver mine first operated in 1910 and now owned by the University in its School of Mineral Industry. We met Tury Anderson, who filed a claim (forfeited by previous owners who stopped working it) in 1947, and has been mining there ever since. He says that the materials go to Montana to be smelted, with a net profit of about a thousand dollars a ton. Tury is retired now, serves in the State Legislature, and helps instruct students at the mine.

Another great trip was to the Permafrost Tunnel, the short name for the U.S. Army Cold Region's Research and Engineering Laboratory's site for research into various means of tunneling through frozen silts and gravels. Permafrost underlies a great part of interior and northern Alaska, and in the Fairbanks area, the summer thaw depth seldom exceeds two feet, with permafrost extending to depths in excess of 100 feet.

Some large ice wedges that we saw in the tunnel started forming at least 33,000 years ago, and have been frozen since that time. Fossil remains that have been found in similar places include mastodon, wooly mammoth, Pleistocene horse, and large-horned bison.

The tunnel is excavated down at an angle through the silty drifted soil to frozen gravel, and is kept at a constant temperature of 5 degrees C, or 22 degrees F, by refrigeration. (Permafrost is defined as ground, either soil or rock, permanently below 0 degrees C.) It has an odor resembling a barn yard due to the decaying of organic matter in the muck that was deposited unfrozen.

The need for research in this area is obvious when one visits here. There are expensive homes, built where there was supposedly no permafrost, that have almost collapsed in the middle, and a road near the University is about to accommodate only one-way traffic because of a stretch that's sinking.

"Drunken forests" are a fairly common sight, all caused by the formation of ice wedges in the frozen silts, with the top of the ice wedge level with the top of the permafrost. Permafrost melts when the ground cover is removed, and the ice wedges also melt, leaving a hole large enough for a cow to fall into if the ground cover is taken off. It was all very interesting, and good that we were warned to wear warm clothing.

Another field trip took us to visit a large dredge, still owned by U.S. Smelting and Refining Co., and although it hasn't been used for about 20 years, it could be moved and reactivated if there were reason to do so. I had seen pictures of gold dredges, but didn't realize how large one could be.

On the same day, we learned about placer mining (pronounced *plasser)* when we watched a sluicing operation going on about 20 miles out of town. It is a three-man operation, and with the aid of a big cat, a high pressure hose, and a long sluice box, they do quite well with seven claims to work.

All of these claims have been worked before. Gold was discovered in this area in 1902, so that era accounted for much exploration along the creeks, and from 1928 through 1951 there was a large scale operation going on, during which 540 million tons of material were handled in this area alone. The high price of gold in recent years has made it worthwhile to rework these claims.

So, of course, we had to try our luck at gold panning. Besides a lot of sore muscles from squatting on the creek bank, we managed to retrieve a few dollars worth of gold.

*Gold panning, taught by an expert.*

We felt that we had earned our lunch at the Chatanika Gold Camp, which is now a fine eating place. Fine in my terms, because they haven't changed the looks of it at all—still the old-type corrugated tin-covered buildings. Worn floors and tables, combined with old pictures, mementos, and great hospitality, transported us back in time to the mining days.

You might be interested in knowing that the Geophysical Institute of the University of Alaska is the world center for research on the subject of the aurora borealis and the optics of polar atmospheres. Our lecture on that subject (with slides) was fascinating.

There is also a NASA satellite tracking station nearby, as well as an Early Warning System here.

In July, Fairbanks celebrates its Golden Days, commemorating the discovery of gold in 1902 by Felix Pedro. What a day! The big event was a parade that must have had 50 floats, 6 bands, 40 horses, 30 antique cars, 100 representatives of the Military (Fort Wainwright and Eielson Ail Force Base) with equipment, and thousands of people all ages and descriptions lining the streets.

Aside from the Army and Air Force personnel, who apparently aren't allowed to smile, everyone involved seemed to be having a great time. Considering that Fairbanks is the center for the entire interior of the State, the crowds weren't such a surprise, but the exuberance and fun of it was.

The next big event in Fairbanks was the exciting and colorful World Eskimo-Indian Olympics. It started 20 years ago, with support from Wein Airways and the Fairbanks Chamber of Commerce. Competitors in the beginning came from neighboring towns, but now it has spread to include some Canadian groups as well. It was so successful that sponsorship was taken over by the *Tundra Times* (Alaska's only Native newspaper) in 1970. In 1976 it became a nonprofit organization.

Competition is unique, in that it is fierce as well as friendly. But more important, the games have been played for many centuries, requiring strength, agility, balance, endurance, and concentration— necessary skills for survival in this harsh environment. It's also a way of passing on their Native heritage from one generation to thc ncxt.

What impressed me the most, besides the beautiful clothing, was the great feeling among the Native people for one another. Lots of happy reunions, with much hugging and chattering in their own languages. Eskimos, in particular, are well known for their affectionate dispositions. This was particularly evident at the Olympics, which were held at the University of Alaska gym, as the small children were free to roam and everyone looked out for them.

Competition included a variety of unusual events, including: The blanket toss: depending on the skill of the pullers, contestants have been tossed as high as 28 feet. To land on their feet on the *oogruk* (bearded seal) blanket requires considerable skill. The ear pull: with a 3-foot piece of heavy string tied into a loop and hooked over one ear, each contestant sits on the floor facing his opponent and tries to pull the other one over. The four men carry: each contestant attempts to carry 600 pounds as far as he can. The weights are people, one on each side and one in front and in back. This was a grueling test! The high kicks: both one-footed and two-footed, these are fascinating to watch. Both men and women entered these races, and were kicking (with both feet off the floor at the same time) heights up to 7 feet 4

*The Chilkat Dancers ready to perform at the Eskimo-Indian Olympics, held every year at the gym of the University of Alaska in Fairbanks.*

inches. The greased pole walk: just what it says.

The dances were most colorful, with Eskimo, Athabascan, and Aleut groups represented. The fish-cutting contest and seal-skinning contest are self-explanatory. Speed is the thing, and the women took the honors in both events with their handy *ulu* knives. The seal, both skin and meat, and the fish, are given away. There was a storytelling contest that I missed, unfortunately. It was going on during the other events, so I had to make a choice.

It was great fun to eat Eskimo Ice Cream, which used to be made from whale blubber, but now is made with Crisco whipped to a light consistency, sweetened to taste, and filled with salmonberries and blueberries—very good and very filling.

There were other things going on, too, and of course, the crowning of the Queen as the climax. She was judged as much on her knowledge of her own Native culture as on her beauty and attire.

The Eskimo Queen candidates were dressed in traditional fur parkas made of such unusual furs as otter bellies combined with seal, polar bear, and other furs elaborately designed and decorated. Athabascans wore the moose-hide or caribou-skin dresses decorated with beautiful beadwork, which is more familiar to us.

Eskimo women in general wear the *kuspuk*, which is a long sleeved, gingham print dress with a hood and a deep ruffle on the bottom, worn over slacks most of the time. The parka (in the old days called *parki*) can be made of any material desired from heavy cotton to velveteen to furs. The ruff around the face is customarily of wolf or wolverine, as these are the only furs that don't frost up with the wearer's breath. After seeing so many attractive ones, I recalled that a friend I had made in Fort Yukon was an excellent parka maker, so I bought some material and sent it to her. My Christmas gift to myself.

The most fun was the opportunity to visit with the participants, and especially the elders, who were enjoying themselves so much. They are highly venerated in both the Eskimo and Indian societies, and the oldest couple at the celebration was a charming gentleman, aged 105, and wife of 90. It was two days of good times.

# CHAPTER 3

# Far Away Places with Strange-Sounding Names

# Solo on the Yukon

A 2½-hour flight from Fairbanks on a Twin Otter (15 passengers) took me north to the Eskimo village of Kotzebue. It was discovered by Otto von Kotzebue in 1816 during a scientific trip for Russia, and was even then an active trading center for furs, skins, and tools. It was called Kikiktagruk at that time.

The village of Kotzebue has a magnificent view, with mountains along the coast to the north and west, and the ocean beyond. The sun is shining for the second day in a row, bringing the dogs out to sit on top of their houses, and the children to play in the puddles.

This is true tundra country, with no trees at all—only willows and other small vegetation. Water birds are prolific, with so much of the land covered by water, and gulls, terns, ducks, and jaegers abound. The Kobuk and the Noatak Rivers flow into the Sound near Kotzebue, and

*Eskimos hanging "squaw candy" to dry. Cut in strips, this salmon is similar to our jerky.*

this is the center for many smaller villages in the area. Subsistence hunting provides seal and beluga whale for winter eating, and salmon are drying on racks to fill in the diet.

Kotzebue is also a thriving commercial fishing center, with five processing plants where the chum salmon are either frozen or packed out fresh by plane.

The fishing boats are about 20 feet long, made from heavy plywood, and are powered by anything from a 35-horsepower motor to a 200-horsepower motor.

For the past two days the wind has been blowing up waves a good three or four feet high, and last evening when I turned in (my little brown tent firmly staked and tied against the gale along the shore), I noticed an overturned boat tangled in the nets that were anchored about 150 yards from shore. It was obvious with my binoculars that there were no people around, in or out of the water. In the morning I learned that three men had gone overboard when the boat swamped in the wind and had become tangled in the net. Other boats were watching and went immediately to their rescue.

Kotzebue is also the center for people of the Park Service who administer the eleven million acres of Park and National Monument lands in the area. That includes Cape Krusenstern, the Kobuk River Sand Dunes, the Gates to the Arctic, the Noatak River, and the Bering Land Bridge. We all hope their "management" means "let it be," not develop it! At Cape Krusenstern, there are 114 different ridges that have built up over the past 5,000 years in a natural beach-building process, and archaeologists are finding evidence of habitation from thousands of years ago. The earliest carbon-dated stone tools and artifacts in the area near the Kobuk River place human habitation there for at least the past 12,500 years.

All this fits in with the theory that originally the continents of Asia and North America were connected, and the earliest people to settle in the Americas came over the Bering Land Bridge from Siberia to spread out over the country. The Noatak River is the largest complete river system remaining in the United States in a condition totally unaltered by man, so it's good to have most of it in a National

Park. These areas are set up to allow subsistence hunting, fishing, and trapping by the Native population and others who depend on it for their livelihood.

Because Kotzebue has no source of logs for home building, there are only a few cabin-type buildings left, dating from around 1900. It's a plywood community now. The Society of Friends missionaries were instrumental in the early education of the Eskimos here, arriving in the late 1800s, and theirs is one of eleven faiths represented in this town of 3,000, although I didn't see very many going to church.

*Wooly Mammoth tusks decorate an old log building in Kotzebue. These and other prehistoric fossils are occasionally uncovered in the spring when the high waters undercut the banks of the rivers.*

In this harsh environment there are no gardens, although the weeds grow in profusion. There are a number of state and federal offices here, a large (for Alaska) airfield, one hotel ($80 per night), and to bring the Eskimos completely into the twentieth century, a new Dairy Queen that can seat up to 100 people.

These Eskimos are Inupiat, and speak an interesting guttural-type language. Except for the very old, almost everyone is bilingual, and even the smallest children are being brought up with both languages. Further south the Eskimos are Yup'ik. They are all friendly and gentle people.

This is the first community I've see where they have utilized the empty oil drums to advantage. They have become a part of their shoreline erosion control program, and must be effective, as the barrels embedded in the gravel-stone beach along the ocean front are slowly rusting away.

One evening, as I sat watching the sun heading down toward the distant mountains, a young fellow from the Park Service asked me if I would care to join him in a double kayak ride. Not one to refuse that kind of proposition, I joined him and we took off, amid a hundred ducks, on the lagoon where the seaplanes land. It was quiet and beautiful, with the rosy violet hues of the sunset growing brighter as the time went by.

We stirred up a group of phalaropes, native to this area. I learned some of the habits of this unusual water bird, which circles and turns on itself in an odd way while diving for food. The female is the colorful one, and the male incubates the young while the female gathers food. Truly a liberated (or hen-pecked?) bird family.

Because I was eager to visit a smaller Eskimo community, a new friend, Terry, who will be teaching in Nome this fall, and I jumped aboard an Islander plane for an hour's flight to the island of Shishmaref.

Another friendly village, only much smaller than ones I previously visited. People started conversations, invited us into their homes for coffee or tea, and seemed to enjoy visitors.

Shishmaref is an isolated island village about 150 miles northwest of Nome, and is a settlement that relies primarily on subsistence hunting, fishing, and food gathering.

As we got out of our small plane we realized that something special was going on. Everyone was hurrying around, the women and girls in their bright colored *kuspuks* (a lightweight parka worn by

Eskimo women in the summer), and the men looking ready for winter. It was an overcast day, with a high wind and a pounding surf of four or five feet. We soon discovered that many were leaving by boat to travel about 25 miles north on the sheltered side of the island to go berrying and moose hunting.

Fortunately, everyone didn't leave. Among those who remained were two artists who were doing commissioned works in bone and wood for museums and galleries, which, when available, sell for anywhere from one to four thousand dollars. Their home is here, but they also have a studio in Seattle for most of the winter.

Another almost world-famous person lives here: Herbie Nayokpuk, who has placed in the famous 1,048-mile Iditarod Dogsled Race for many years. He was a guest at the White House for Reagan's inauguration and had to get himself into top hat, white tie, and tails! From the picture, his wife looked charming in her ball gown, but Herbie said he was a bit uncomfortable. Full dress isn't a part of Native Eskimo culture! We had the pleasure of meeting his wife and a number of his children and grandchildren.

The Iditarod Dogsled Race leaves Anchorage each year on the first Saturday in March for the start of the world's longest and toughest dogsled race. The goal is Nome, over 1,000 miles away, and the trail takes the challengers over tundra, rivers, mountains, and the ice-locked sea coast.

The men and women who take part in this grueling race are a unique lot, and Herbie is no exception. He owns about 50 sled dogs and already knows which ones will run in next year's race. They are staked out on chains by their houses in the vicinity of our tent, and we are besieged by any number of puppies who are running loose—even chewing up my tent fly! These dogs "sing," as do those belonging to the Athabascans.

The Native villages of Alaska have had the opportunity to vote on whether or not to allow liquor to be sold in their communities. Shishmaref hasn't voted yet, but there doesn't seem to be as much of a problem here as in the Athabascan villages.

Life in these isolated areas can only go on if everyone helps every-

*Shishmaref Eskimos about to launch
a fishing boat in the Bering Sea.*

one else, and we saw a good example of that as so many families prepared to go out to their camps. They travel in large sea-worthy boats with good-sized outboards, and when a man wants to get his boat ready, all his friends come to help him turn the boat over, put the motor on, and move it to where it is loaded and launched.

Vehicles in this village consist of one broken-down flatbed truck that meets all planes, another pickup truck, and a half dozen three-wheeled Honda RVs that must have been designed for use in the villages. The only street is planked with old corrugated-type steel connecting surfacing that was used for instant landing strips in the Pacific during World War II. But most of these have become disconnected. Everything else is sand, some grass, and marsh. They say it takes hundreds of years for a scar on the tundra to grow back, so I'm glad the RVs only go where they need to.

Nome, the first incorporated city in Alaska, is an interesting town with history that goes back to 1898, when gold was found in the area. It was first discovered in Anvil Creek, which attracted a few hundred people, but when gold was discovered mixed with the ocean sands, the population jumped to over 15,000 by 1901. The ease with which the beach sand could be sorted from the gold, as compared to mining in the Klondike, for instance, and the simplicity of transportation to and from being so much easier, it was no wonder that thousands of men (and women) stampeded to the "golden sands of Nome."

The restrictions were interesting. There were no claims as such on the beach, and if a miner left the spot he picked, another was free to take it over. The amount of space allotted to one person was all that could be encircled with an outstretched shovel handle.

*A modern, portable gold dredge working the beaches of Nome, where gold was first discovered early in this century.*

Today gold mining provides a major source of employment in the summer through the Alaska Gold Company. "Bessie" (Dredge #5) still remains the largest operating gold dredge in the world. The recent revival of Nome's gold dredges brings in several millions of dollars during operating season.

Fort Davis, several miles south of town, was first established by the government to keep peace among the miners in the early days, similar to several others I've visited. However, the pattern usually followed that by the time the fort was built, the stampede was over and the need for it minimal.

There have been two fires that all but destroyed Nome, one in 1905 and another in 1934, but each time the town was rebuilt. There are still many of the original structures standing as landmarks of the past, however. The population now is about 3,000, 75 per cent of which is Eskimo. It supports a local junior college, as well as a high school and grade school of about 400 students each. There are several hundred miles of roads leading out of Nome to smaller communities or mines, but no connection "outside" except by air or water.

Barge traffic handles most of the materials that come and go from Nome, and although everything must be offloaded half a mile out because of shallow water, there is a lot of shipping going on. People in isolated areas on the coast or up the rivers buy their year's (or at least a season's) supply of food wholesale from Seattle, to be delivered by ship and then barged to its destination. These barge orders offer a considerable saving. In Nome today milk is selling for $5.85 per gallon. Obviously, people use dry milk here! The apples we bought cost 75 cents apiece and came from New Zealand!

Nome is also a tourist town, with special air fares and tours offered through travel agencies. Every day we see a different group being escorted to the points of interest. Combined with the Native population, the crews from the ships, and the miners, there is quite a mix of nationalities and interests.

One day Terry and I were fortunate to have a car lent to us by a friend, and we drove several miles out to visit friends of hers who have built a new home by a small river. Beautifully designed. Later we drove the road north along the beach for many miles. It was a glorious sunny day, and we saw all kinds of interesting things along the way. The usual abandoned machinery rusting away in the salt air, along with dead walrus washed up on the beach, minus heads. They are slaughtered for their ivory, giving the Natives one of only a few cash incomes they enjoy. Fortunately, the walrus herds are, if anything, too plentiful—otherwise the waste would be intolerable. Another interesting thing we saw was a huge red gold mining contraption, on wheels, that had about a 14-foot diameter. It obviously was a gold digging and sluicing machine, but we were sorry not to see it working.

Nome radio hasn't too much going for it, but the Hot Line program is interesting. Every station serving the bush, both in Alaska and Canada, has a communications service for anyone who wants to get messages out. Some of them are very personal, some happy, some sad, but it provides good service.

After spending several pleasant days in Nome, it was time for me to return to Fairbanks for the start of a backpacking trip in the Brooks Range on August 8. This was the only scheduled thing I had arranged prior to my arrival in Alaska.

CHAPTER 4

# Packing Up
# and
# Rafting Down

BACKPACKING AND RAFTING IN THE BROOKS RANGE.

**Day One:** Departure day dawned bright and sunny in Fairbanks as I joined four other backpackers at the airport for the first leg of our plane trip into the Brooks Range. We had met the evening before to get acquainted and talk about last-minute details over an excellent Chinese dinner.

The leaders of the trip are a young couple, Carol and Jim, who have been taking trips on their own for some time, and now do three or four trips a summer as a business. The other members of the group are two girls: one, Monica from Chicago, on her annual two-week vacation; and the other, Lois from California, a nurse practitioner taking a year off to travel. It's a small and congenial group.

The Brooks Range runs east and west in Arctic Alaska, and is truly one of the last great wilderness areas in the world. It is a harsh and

*These are the friends who shared the hiking adventure,*
*including the couple who organized the trip.*

forbidding environment, with jagged granite spires, wild storms, and immense open space as well. There is only one small village, Anaktuvuk Pass, in the entire area. The Prudhoe Bay pipeline and the haul road accompanying it cut across the mountains at Anaktuvuk.

The first leg of our air travel was a commercial flight on a small plane to Bettles, which is a small community at the extreme south end of the central Brooks Range. Low clouds and bad flying weather kept us on the ground in a state of uncertainty for about four hours, so we spent the time talking with the park rangers of this newly created Gates to the Arctic National Park, and visiting the sod-roofed trading post.

The next leg of our trip was by chartered seaplane, a Beaver, which we had quite a time loading because of the swift current in the river. This is the north fork of the Koyokuk River, which we will eventually be coming down by rubber raft at the end of our trip. After many hundreds of miles it makes its way to the Yukon, and then to the ocean.

We were shown a fine example of the Beaver's high performance ability as the pilot jockeyed us up the river valley under the clouds, with mountains often very close on either side. Craggy peaks, swift streams coming from the summits, and rain clouds hanging very low created a variety of patterns as we followed the winding river to its source, Summit Lake. To go further would take us across the divide into rivers flowing into the Arctic Ocean. This is the area described by Bob Marshal, who explored these rivers and mountains in the 1930s for the National Park Service, and who named the twin peaks on either side of the river Gates to the Arctic. His book, *Alaska Wilderness,* is a fine one to read about this area, as there have been no changes in it since he traveled here.

The plane set us down on the lake and we quickly found out what the Arctic tundra really is. The answer is *wet.* Because we were so late, our only wish was to find a dry spot to put up tents and get supper, which involved a short hike, but what a beautiful spot! The small quiet lake reflects the jagged peaks, and the shades of green and brown of the tiny tundra plants add unexpected color. No trees, except small willows along the river.

Lots of birds—loons, terns, and jaegers so far, and eight Dall sheep across the river and high on a hillside. Good dinner and to bed early.

**Day Two:** Mostly rainy drizzle, but no hard rains. Stayed in camp and took a day hike up an interesting canyon. Saw three bull caribou on the opposite hill—such magnificent creatures! They were carrying the largest racks I've ever seen. There were more sheep, but scarcely visible without binoculars. To bed at 11:00 after a fine dinner and an evening of storytelling. Temperature is 46 degrees.

**Day Three:** The first day of hiking with full packs. Mine weighs 45 pounds and is probably the lightest of the group, as I managed to pack with a minimum amount of gear. The only thing we don't skimp on is wool, however. In this climate we need wool socks, wool gloves, hat, and shirts. Hiking anywhere involves fording streams, climbing rocks, scrambling in gravel, or fighting the indomitable sedge tussock. You can't walk on them (they throw you off balance), and you can't walk between them (the sphagnum moss disguises the depth of the water and you may sink in up to your knees). So, with occasional mountain sides for relief, we only traveled about eight miles before setting up camp.

**Day Four:** Can you imagine opening your eyes in the morning to see 15 caribou greeting you from several hundred yards away? What a beautiful sight! They are a very curious animal, as we found out later in the day. They eventually circled all the way around us, stopping every few minutes to gaze intently in our direction. The bulls are in prime coat at this time of year, with racks that must be four or five feet from tip to tip. There are many caribou herds in Alaska, and these are a part of the Arctic herd of 242,000.

Later in the afternoon, after a precipitous descent down a deep gorge, we followed the river through willow thickets for quite a while. To let the bears know we were there, we talked and sang. Lois was calling, "Bear, bear, here we come," and sure enough, very soon and only about 30 feet away, there was a young grizzly looking directly at us. In a moment he turned and loped away, and after we had gained our composure by realizing that he was too large to have a mother

*Hiking along the north fork of the Koyukuk River*
*in the Central Brooks Range in Arctic Alaska.*

protecting him, we enjoyed watching him run up the hillside and across a small cliff, silhouetted against the sky. He was about the size of our medium black bears, his fur was lighter than most grizzlies, and it looked silky as it rippled and waved as he ran.

Our campsite for the night borders a fairly large river that we'll have to cross, and judging from the number of blueberries, bear-berries, and some chokecherries, we must be in prime bear country. The barren-ground grizzly, as opposed to those in the parks, need a hundred square miles of habitat for each animal. In the Brooks Range they are totally unaccustomed to people, and tend to depart as quickly as they can.

**Day Five:** Rain all night. I'm still unconvinced that this is a semi-arid country with minimal rainfall per year. They all say, "This year is unusual." It was a surprise, however, to look out in the morning to find a beautiful powdered-sugar sprinkling of snow on the mountains, made more striking by its contrast to the black rock. But I'm not ready for winter camping!

As we are in no way hurried to get to the spot on the river where our two rafts are being dropped off by plane, there seemed to be good reason to stay over in this beautiful location and hike without packs today. The colors of the tundra are more impressive every day, and as fall approaches, the willows and small cottonwood along the streams are turning yellow and red—there is a small, wintergreen-type plant whose leaves turn a brilliant red over large patches of hillside, there are many varieties of fungus that come in assorted colors, and in between, the inevitable caribou moss, which grows in all the north country, caribou or not. Considering that nothing on the mountains grows over three or four inches high, it's a lot of color.

The highest elevations in the Brooks Range are only 9,000 or 10,000 feet, but because we are in the Arctic, the tree line is at only 3,000 feet here, instead of the 15,000 in some of the Rockies.

Today we saw more Dall sheep, two eagles, and any number of parka squirrels, so named because the Eskimos made parkas of the fur. And our campsite was overrun by Arctic hares, whose coats were already changing from brown to white. To top off the evening, after a fine dinner and good conversation, at about the time we were thinking of turning in, we saw a tremendous bull moose on the other side of the river. He was feeding in the willow brush, and very slowly meandered about a quarter of a mile within our sights. He seemed larger than our Ontario moose, and I was sorry not to be able to photograph him. It was too late in the evening.

**Day Six:** The powdered sugar on the mountains has turned into frosting, and I guess winter has begun for good. Only a few drizzles today, and enough sun to bring out the fall colors of the mountains. Many small streams to cross in ice water above our boot tops, and one river that required considerable concentration because of the fast water. Beautiful rainbows today. Mount Doonerak, the highest of the surrounding peaks, came in view in the afternoon. The Numamiut people, who live nearby in Anaktuvuk, have many superstitions about it, which is understandable, as it is a craggy, black, forbidding mountain that is apparently

*View from a mountain of the Koyukuk.*

unclimbable.

There are a few places along the rivers in the southern Brooks Range where small black spruce grow, and we were able to find a camping place near such a spot, so we had a large campfire that was much appreciated in the cool weather.

**Day Seven:** No rain today—a first. Cold, but invigorating for our last day of hiking. At breakfast time we caught a parka squirrel feasting on the blueberries we were saving for breakfast. He was quite tame, but a bit flustered when we tried to shoo him away. All the animals seem to be more curious than afraid of us. Even a huge porcupine didn't bother to stop nibbling on his cottonwood branch as I walked up to him. Besides being camped on a willow-covered gravel bar that has provided browse for moose, we apparently have dropped in on a true *Watership Down* home of many dozens of the intriguing

Arctic hare. They are so investigative that if we sit still they will come almost to our feet, but usually in the late evening.

Today we alternated hiking through the tussocks (but by no stretch of the imagination should it be termed "hiking," rather "wallowing"), with long stretches on gravel bars and some side-hill walking. Tonight we are camped at the raft site, where two four-man rafts and next week's supply of food were flown in and cached high in the trees for safety. It was a welcome sight to find them. Temperature down to 38 degrees tonight.

**Days Seven and Eight:** Two days in this beautiful spot—great! The first started with blueberry pancakes for brunch, followed by a reorganization of food and gear from backpacking to rafting. Also a time for washing clothes and bathing (very quickly). It was a welcome leisurely day. The second day we did a 2,500-foot climb in the hope of seeing Lake Marshall, a small alpine lake nearby. The ascent was mostly boulder climbing, with some talus slopes that had to be crossed. These are made up of the disintegrated rock that falls down the mountains to form sometimes very large, triangular slopes that are somewhat unstable for walking. Also just enough elementary rock climbing to be a challenge. When we came close to the last ascent it proved to be too difficult by the route we had used, as we were faced with a snow-covered headwall. Jim did climb up and over to see the lake, but he must share some traits with the mountain goat!

During our lunch stop it snowed on us and the temperature probably never got above 40 degrees for most of the day. Invigorating. We passed a number of falls on the way up, which were spectacular, and found many old glacial ice formations that never melt from one year to the next. The views from the top were breathtaking.

The day ended with Jim hurrying back to camp to have dinner ready for us when we arrived, quite late. A driftwood fire finished off the day and five weary people slept well.

**Day Nine:** The first day of rafting. Jim and Carol had said that the only tricky part of the river is the first day. They were so right! We were no sooner loaded and off than the two rafts plunged into a mass of whitewater and rocks, the likes of which I've never before been in. But a raft isn't a canoe, and with a little urging it usually managed to slide off anything, except the all-too-prevalent shallow gravel bars, where the only solution is to get out and wade in the ice-cold water.

One black bear and many beaver joined us briefly as we floated by. No signs of any people anywhere since we started the trip, except for the sound of a few small planes overhead. It's mind-boggling to think of all these millions of acres of wilderness that is rightfully being preserved as Gates of the Arctic National Park, because it really does belong to the grizzlies, the wolves, the sheep, and the caribou.

Tomorrow we'll have to patch the bottom of one of the rafts.

**Days 10 and 11:** Both days on the river. Cold weather, snow in the air, and heavy clouds moving across the sky each day. The current is swift, but no more rapids, and with a strong wind from the north we made good time both days. Sheltered campsites along the river are rare, but now that we're almost a hundred miles south, we are entering a more forested area, and can find stands of spruce and cottonwood. Strange to see cottonwood so far north, as I associate it with the southwest canyon country, though these trees will never reach as large a size.

The rocks, both large and small, are of such variety and beauty that it's a temptation to bring home a pack full. Think I'll have to at least send some samples. We now have added wolf and fox tracks to our list, but most animals seem to be able to keep out of our sight.

Our meals have been excellent. Dinners are one-pot meals of dried ingredients with fresh onions, carrots, or cabbage added, and now that we are rafting and have had our food supplies replenished, we can be more luxurious than when we had to carry it all on our backs. Carol made up desserts of honey bars, date bars, and such things ahead of time, and a few weeks in foil doesn't seem to bother them. Lunches are mostly crackers, cheese, dried fruit, and cookies, and breakfasts are standard granola, oatmeal, and other cereals, with occasional pancakes and (once) eggs.

It was interesting to stop and see a small cabin that a friend of Jim's had built a few years ago, where they had spent a summer prospecting for gold. Good to find that all the equipment (chain saw, tools, etc.) was safe in the cache, and that the cabin was still supplied with emergency food.

Days are getting shorter now, and it actually is dark around midnight, for a change.

**Days 12 and 13:** Hurray for a sunny day! Thinking it would be warm on the river, we all dressed accordingly, only to find that there was a cold wind blowing against us. The leaves are turning more every day, and the colors are reminiscent of Wisconsin. No maples, though. The river widened out today and is deeper, so we no longer get our feet wet, which is much appreciated.

The most exciting events of these two days have been the northern lights. Seeing them against the evening sky is different, and we continued watching until quite late. They were multicolored and more vivid than I've ever seen before. Did you know that the aurora has been measured and tracked by geophysicists at the University of Alaska, and they have found that the display we see in the northern hemisphere is simultaneously duplicated in the southern polar

*After the hiking, a restful week of rafting
back to the town of Bettles.*

skies? Amazing. It was good to see a few stars again—the first I've seen since early June, as the summer night skies are never dark enough. Good sleeping without a tent, but freezing temperatures.

**Day 14:** Last day on the river, and it turned out to be a perfect one. We were in no hurry, so floated all day, luxuriating in the sunshine and taking a long lunch stop combined with a hike in the afternoon. To celebrate our last dinner, we cooked two pizzas for supper (no mix). Quite a feat over two small backpacking stoves. And to top it all off, the sunset was a magnificent display of color.

The trip back to Fairbanks was uneventful, all of us not too eager to get back into city living, but by the time the plane landed, we had made plans to meet the following night for dinner. Our two weeks had brought us all together into a very close and warm relationship, and I'm sure we will see one another again.

It was a never-to-be-forgotten experience for me.

# CHAPTER 5

# Denali — Grandeur on a Large Scale

# Solo on the Yukon

Another week in Fairbanks has been one of reorganizing my gear, enjoying last visits with a number of new friends, helping Celia and Ginny, and in general getting ready to leave in a few days. The weather has been perfect, after a brief cold spell—which was just enough to nudge Alaskans in this area to thinking about how soon winter will be here. Lots of activity in the wood gathering, splitting, and stacking areas, but I feel for all these people who endure temperatures as low as –50 degrees to –60 degrees every winter without the advantage of any oak or maple to burn. They are acutely conscious of the need for adequate insulation, and the log cabin I'm staying in has outside walls 18 inches thick, and not many windows except on the south.

The gardens, after soaking up so much extra light during the long summer days, are now giving up their produce, and most people are trying to squeeze in time for harvesting, freezing, and canning in order to save spending large amounts of money for high-priced fruits and vegetables during the winter. Most people buy staple foods only two or three times during the year in quantity, raise chickens, shoot moose (or have friends who do), fish a lot or buy and freeze it when the price is low, and manage to combat the high prices quite effectively.

A last-minute visit which I will remember as a high spot of my time in Fairbanks was when Celia, Ginny, and I were invited to the small cabin home of Mary Shields and John Manthei. John is the brother of Sue Pucci of Manitowish Waters, Wisconsin, who had suggested that I get in touch with them, not only because he is her brother, but because of the fascinating lifestyle they have. Both John and Mary believe that life should be lived right now, and that working an eight-hour day and a five-day week for fifty weeks a year isn't conducive to that end. So both are busy a part of the year, John with his own custom cabinet making, furniture making, and one-of-a-kind bowls turned from burls that have a most unusual grain. He has also built and furnished the two cabins they own. The one we visited is about ten miles out of Fairbanks and can only be reached by a mile and a half of rather obscure trail. That's their summer cabin. Their winter cabin is even further out and more inaccessible. One reason

*Mary Shields and John Manthei in front of
their summer house outside of Fairbanks.*

for this is that they own two dog teams, and much of their life revolves around them. At the moment they have ten adult dogs— mostly Huskies, and about eight pups for sale, and as soon as the snow flies, John and Mary move to their winter cabin and give up working in favor of dogsledding. Mary works three summer months for the Alaska Fish and Game Department.

She ran the Iditarod race several years ago. Not many women do —it's over a thousand miles of sledding through the mountains and across the rivers from Anchorage to Nome. She is the only person that anyone knows of who ran the race and then turned around and ran it backwards almost all the way. Two reasons for that. One was finances, or lack of it, as most people fly their teams back from Nome to wherever they live, and the other was that Mary wanted to visit with the people who were so good to her on the way. The villagers along the route take in the contestants when they need food and rest, sometimes turning one of their own children out of a bed to do so, and Mary wanted to be able to do more than rush in and rush out. John has been dogsledding for many years in many parts of Alaska, and it was fascinating to hear some of the stories they had to tell. Both are in their mid thirties, so I'm not talking about old timers except in the realm of experience. They have invited me back for Thanksgiving, which is a big dogsledding holiday for them, and I don't think I'll be able to refuse.

Interesting fact relating to the Husky dogs: there is a large group of people in Fairbanks who are involved in spinning, dying, and weaving dog fur, and a natural color knitted hat that I bought my son Ken for his birthday was knitted from part wool and part fur from a friend of Mary's Husky dogs. They are incredibly soft. Mary has written a number of articles for *Alaska Magazine,* and has been heard over National Public Radio many times.

So it will be goodbye to Fairbanks, at least until snow time. I will miss Ginny Wood and Celia Hunter, who have accepted me as part of their family. I'll miss their stories of the early days of flying in Alaska, such as helping to start the flying tour business with nothing to provide even the minimum of comfort for the patrons, and landing DC-3s on the narrow beach of Shishmaref "just for the heck of it." I'll miss their keen insight into the problems of the world and their comments on current political and environmental concerns.

So now to continue with my own adventures and impressions. Last week when I was hitching back to my friend Celia's house from downtown Fairbanks, I got a ride with a girl in a van, who in response to my comments about the weather and just having returned from the Brooks Range, abruptly said, "You must be Helen." Quite a coincidence. She was house-sitting for the leaders of my backpacking trip and was hoping to join Lois and me for our proposed trip to Katmai National Park following our visit to Denali. Katmai closed too soon, so we changed plans and came up with a good alternative—a trip on the Alaska Ferry.

Susan (the girl with the van) drove us to Denali, where we met Carol and Jim (backpacking leaders), who were on the proverbial busman's holiday, and joined them for some hiking in the park. Our campsite wasn't the best; it was Labor Day weekend and the choice sites were already taken, and we ended up sharing a site with two fellows who had just left their summer jobs in a fish cannery in Kodiak after saving $3,000 apiece in a couple of months. Interesting to hear their comments.

Neither pictures nor words are adequate to describe Denali Park and its majestic scenery and wildlife. I'll attempt it, but first, some background. The entire area is dominated by Mount McKinley. No other mountain in the world, not even in the Himalayas, rises so high above its own base to stand in such lofty isolation over its neighbors. The summit, crowned by twin peaks, reaches an altitude of 20,320 feet, which is 16,000 feet above its surrounding mountains, so it's a small wonder that the Indians of Alaska called it Denali—the great one.

Setting off this majestic peak are 100 miles of the Alaska Range with no peaks less than 10,000 feet, and another 480 miles in the remainder of the curved range that forms a natural barrier between Anchorage on the coastal lowlands and the interior to the north.

The vegetation consists of spruce, alder, willow, and birch in the river and creek valleys; taiga or tundra on the higher slopes (the word *taiga* comes from a Russian word meaning little sticks; trees in the taiga areas are small); and, of course, many varieties of rock in the mountains themselves. The mountains vary in shape from rounded domes to craggy peaks, and from bare rock with snow cover to complete vegetation. There are many active glaciers in the park, which are the source of the headwaters of the Susitna, the Kuskokwin, and the Yukon Rivers, and one, the Muldrow Glacier, was clearly visible from the park road.

It's hard to believe that when Alaska was purchased from the Russians in 1867, the Alaska Range had not been explored, and the

*View from the road in Denali National Park.*

only reference to mountains in the interior was made by Baron von Wrangell, who showed them on his map of 1839. The discovery of gold brought many people to Alaska, and one of them, William Dickey, wrote a glowing account of his travels, describing America's rival to Mount Everest. This was published in the *New York Sun,* and Dickey was instrumental in naming Mount McKinley after William McKinley of Ohio.

By 1910 there was regular traffic through the canyon country of the Nenana River, with the result that in 1914 President Wilson authorized construction of the railroad that was to go from Seward on the south, past Mount McKinley, and on to Fairbanks on the north. In 1917 Wilson signed into law the bill establishing Mount McKinley National Park as an area of 2,500 square miles. This was expanded in 1922, 1932, and again in 1980 under the Alaska Lands Act, so that now the park contains 5.6 million acres, making it roughly the same size as the state of Massachusetts.

The highway between Anchorage, McKinley, and Fairbanks was completed in 1971, making the park available to even more tourists. As a result the McKinley Park Hotel, after burning to the ground in 1972 and being rebuilt, is now trying to accommodate the increasing number of tourists who converge on it each summer.

The Park Service runs shuttle buses the length of the park road and doesn't allow private cars on it except to get to and from a campsite. This cuts down on traffic, and as the animals have no fear of the buses, the possibility of seeing wildlife is enhanced. On our first day we didn't see much—only moose feeding on a stream bed not far from our campsite.

The second day we did a variety of things, including making a visit to the McKinley Park sled dog kennels and a demonstration of the dogs in action with a wheeled sled. The ranger explained a lot about the dogs and the equipment, and we were free to walk around, pet the dogs, and spend as much time as we wished asking questions and looking around.

There is a long history of dogsledding in the park, and as soon as there is sufficient snow the rangers take the teams out on patrol, as it's easier than any other way to check on poachers in the area. They also conduct dogsled tours for winter visitors, as well as backcountry ski tours. I was interested in some scale-model replicas of working sleds, so Lois and I got the name of the retired ranger who made them, promptly telephoned and ordered one apiece, to be delivered around the first of the year. There is an interesting follow-up to this a little later.

Another reason why my interest has been aroused in dogsledding is that the evening before I left Fairbanks I was fortunate to be able to the film *Spirit of the Wind* at the University of Alaska. It was produced by Doyon, Inc. (the Native corporation that geographically includes a great deal of the interior, including Fairbanks), under the label Raven Films. It is the true life story of George Attla, an Eskimo who as a young boy had serious leg surgery over a period of years, leaving him with a fused knee joint. He overcame many difficulties to become a world champion dogsledder.

The movie is extraordinary because there are only a few non-Native people in it, the music was composed and sung by Buffy St. Marie, and it portrays everyday Eskimo village life and the training of dogs so well. There was a rumor that it had earned a Cannes Film Festival award.

Back to Denali: As in all National Parks, there were evening shows depicting various aspects of interest and opening the eyes of the general public to what is surrounding them. We attended one. We also went to the McKinley Park Hotel for afternoon tea, as we didn't want to spend $15 on a dinner, and had a fun time watching how the other half lives.

Tour buses in large numbers, baggage piled 10 feet high, people lined up everywhere waiting for one thing or another—even at the "potty stops" at outhouses along the park highway.

The next day brought my meeting with friends Celia and Ginny from Fairbanks, who, after selling their Camp Denali Lodge, retained cabins that are reached by following the park road the full 90 miles through the park, to just outside its limit on the west side. They also have a cabin just off Alaska Highway 2 about 10 miles from the McKinley Station, on Deneki Lakes. That's were I spent the next night, having said goodbye to Lois and Susan, who are meeting me in Anchorage.

The further note on the dogsled replicas is that Celia and Ginny took me next door to another cabin turned into a house, to meet their friends the Nancarrow family. Bill turned out to be the retired Park Service ranger I had ordered the sled from!

He also works in Caribou antler bone. When we arrived they were up to their elbows in moose meat, which they were preparing to freeze for their winter's meat supply. They have their own generator, so live quite comfortably in the bush. She is also an artist.

After closing up the Deneki Lake cabin the following morning, we drove to Celia and Ginny's A-frame just outside Denali Park. What a beautiful spot, half way up a small mountain, with a great view of Mount McKinley out their front windows! We were joined by a friend of theirs who is a doctor in Anchorage. Later I was treated to a tour around Camp Denali Lodge, which although in a totally different environment, reminded me in many ways of old Camp Minocqua.

In the process of coming and going through the park, the list of animals seen has steadily grown to include 5 grizzly bears, about 10 caribou, 15 or 20 Dall sheep, and several moose.

Add to that the fact that this morning on my way back to take the train the sun was out and Mount McKinley was clearly visible from most of the road. Many visitors come and never have the opportunity to see it because of the clouds. They say the mountain is "out" only about one day in five; I should have good pictures.

*The classic picture of Mt. McKinley, the highest peak in North America, which rises higher above its base than any other mountain in the world. This was taken from Camp Denali.*

CHAPTER 6

# Glaciers
# and
# Special Places

SO THESE HAVE BEEN GREAT DAYS. EVERY ONE BRINGS SOMETHING NEW AND exciting, and now I'm off for another mini adventure in south-east Alaska. Starting in Anchorage, where I was staying with friends of Susan and Lois, we three drove the van to Portage, a distance of about eighty miles along Turnagain Arm of Cook Inlet. So named by Captain Cook during his early explorations because he found no outlet. The area surrounding Anchorage is spectacular, with the coastal mountains and many bays of Cook Inlet providing every kind of recreational opportunity imaginable. At Portage we boarded the Alaska Railroad for a short trip through three tunnels in the Chugach Mountains, ending at the town of Whittier, where we boarded the ferry.

Strange town, Whittier. Built by the Army during World War II, it consists primarily of two many-storied, huge concrete buildings that appear to have very little going for them from the outside. One is abandoned, and the other houses the homes, library, stores, bowling alley, and just about the entire town. Its location and fine harbor on Prince William Sound make it a desirable place to sail or fish from in the summer, but winter must be difficult.

Our ferry was the M/V *Bartlett*, one of the smaller of the fleet, but complete with restaurant, though no reclining deck chairs. We were out for two nights, so slept in our sleeping bags on the top deck or "solarium." The first stop was Valdez, by then rather late in the evening. The city was moved and rebuilt following the earthquake of 1964, and is located across the bay from the terminus of the Alaska pipeline. We arrived at the next stop, Cordova, early the next morning with a twelve-hour layover there. Similar to most towns in the southeast, it is nestled along the shore at the foot of the mountains on a narrow shelf of land. The principal industry is fishing, and the harbor is a mass of hundreds of assorted varieties of fishing craft, from very small but seaworthy gill netters to large purse seiners, to big, highly automated ships requiring a crew of ten or fifteen people. There were only about 2,000 inhabitants, so it didn't take us very long to get acquainted with the town. The library and museum were closed for repairs, so we decided to do a day hike to Crater Lake, which was at the summit of the small mountain behind the town.

True to southern Alaska's usual custom, it began to rain soon after the start of our hike, but it failed to dampen our appreciation of the lush rainforest with its deep mosses, huge ferns, and ancient trees. By the time we reached timberline, with no shelter from the trees, we were soaked in spite of raincoats. The local laundromat provided the solution to our problem, as we were carrying no extra clothes with us, but the dilemma involved in getting out of wet clothes, drying them, and then dressing again in a public place was something to laugh at. Being thoroughly dry, we decided to try out the new swimming pool in town, and after that a dinner in a motel restaurant at the harbor. Then back to the ferry for another short night's sleep before arriving back at Whittier and the train to Portage.

There were many interesting things that we saw along the way, and the Columbia Glacier, with its hundreds of icebergs and face of ice that varies from 150 to 250 feet above the water, was one of the most fascinating. The typical turquoise blue of the ice is due to the reflection and refraction of the light from the compacted ice crystals, and it was a beautiful contrast to the dark colors of the forest and the waters. Columbia Glacier is roughly the size of Rhode Island—41 miles long and about five miles wide at its terminus. It extends as far as 2,300 feet below sea level in places, and is advancing at a rate of 6 feet each day, which is considered very active for a glacier. The ferry approached the wall to within a quarter of a mile, and the Captain's customary assistants when he blew the ship's whistle were a number of the youngest passengers, eager to see if their toot would result in a part of the glacier separating, or "calving," and thundering into the water amid a 200-foot spray. True to form, we watched this happen several times, both on our trip over and on our trip back.

The hundreds of harbor seals resting on the floating ice were not in the least disturbed by either the loud noise or the ship, and we enjoyed almost half an hour of watching the playful pups and their parents. With their big black eyes and black noses, they resemble an oversized puppy dog, and seem to have a great curiosity about the ship. The other exciting viewing was a school of orcas, or killer

*Columbia Glacier, 2½ miles wide and 200 feet high.*

whales. There must have been twenty or thirty playing around the boat while the captain circled to make it easier for us to see them.

We also saw a kittiwake rookery, where hundreds of gull-like birds were resting in the cliffs. Mountains surround Prince William Sound, and many of the islands are hilly and thickly forested. For much of the trip the weather was overcast, giving the vistas a soft, shades-of-grey atmosphere, which was exquisite. Even the rains were soft. Unfortunately, this is the last year that the Alaska Ferry System, which is owned by the state, will be making this run, as the cruise boats have objected to "unfair competition." So we're fortunate to have been able to take such a good trip so inexpensively. The food was good, too.

After a night with friends on top of a mountain overlooking the city of Anchorage, Susan offered to drive me out of town to start my first hitchhiking jaunt. After pricing the airfare from Anchorage to Glacier Bay ($380 round trip, and the bus only $100 cheaper), I decided to hitch to Haines, take the ferry to Juneau, and then fly to Glacier Bay.

The first ride took me to Palmer, just 40 miles out of Anchorage. There was only one reasonable place to wait for a ride, and it was taken by a very nice young man from New Zealand, who was going to Dawson City. I joined him for a while, but after a couple of hours with no luck, decided to go for a meal. When I returned he was gone, and although there was plenty of traffic, most of it was local, and I had another two-hour wait. My luck turned when a young man who was a guide's assistant just in from a moose hunt in the Alaska Range came by. He was ferrying meat and gear from a small airfield near Glenallen to Anchorage, and was glad to have company. It was a five-hour drive, and too late when we got there for me to look up Carl and Gladys Bauers of Woodruff, Wisconsin. I slept that night in the equipment shed belonging to the guide, whose name was Mel. Except for the ghosts inhabiting the 400 pounds of moose meat hanging in there with me, it was a comfortable place to stay—even had a bunk.

A 6:00 a.m. breakfast the next morning at the nearby motel brought me in touch with a gentleman and his son who were traveling by van loaded with the household belongings of the Seattle-bound son. They were heading for the ferry at Haines, as I was, so we had a very pleasant full day of driving through some of the greatest scenery I've ever seen, including a bird's-eye view of Kluane Provincial Park in British Columbia. That's also on my "next-time" list. The road disintegrated for a while, so we didn't arrive in Haines until about 10:00 p.m., which includes a two-hour time change and two trips through customs.

Chilkat Indians lived in the Haines area long before John Muir and S. Hall Young, a missionary, selected the site for a town. The mission was established in 1881, followed by the salmon canneries, mining, and an Army post in 1903. During the Klondike gold rush it was the southern end of the Dalton Trail, a notorious toll road over which goods were transported to the northern settlements.

There is a fine revival in Haines of Chilkat crafts and skills, and a number of local artisans doing good work. The Chilkat Dancers are well known throughout Alaska.

Another attraction, which we missed because of our late arrival, was the great number of bald eagles to be seen along the Chilkat River flats about 20 miles out of town. The river has warm springs running into it, so it never freezes, and is the location of Alaska's last salmon run of the year. As many as 3,000 eagles have been counted there in a single day! November is the peak month, so maybe I can return to see them.

Tonight in a motel in Haines, the first I've been in since I started the trip in June. Didn't like to break my good record, but it was too late at night and too much rain to set up a tent.

The five-hour ferry trip from Haines to Juneau was interesting. The *Malaspina* is one of the larger, more luxurious ferries. I arrived at 11:00 p.m. in the rain, so due to the late hour, the rain, and no Youth Hostel accommodations open, I took a room at the Alaska Hotel. It had been suggested by the purser on the ferry as the best of the two inexpensive hotels in town. (In Alaskan towns that means less than fifty dollars a night.) What a surprise it was! Recently placed on the National Register of Historic Places, it is the oldest operating hotel in Juneau. It opened in 1913 and is an excellent example of the architectural changes between the 19th and 20th centuries. In the early mining days there were boarding houses and rooming houses, but no hotels, so this filled the gap. Conveniently located close to downtown and the docks, it now boasts a Jacuzzi room, a sauna, and antique furnishings in all the rooms. Lots of stained glass, too.

Juneau, at the north end of Alaska's panhandle, is nestled among the islands and mountains of the Gastineau Channel, and is the capitol of Alaska, only accessible by air or boat. Several years ago the state voted to move the capitol to Willow, an almost nonexistent village north of Anchorage, but the voters have failed to support bills for the funding of the project. It would be necessary to build an entire city and government complex from scratch, so the price tag is exorbitant.

Juneau's most famous scenic wonder is the Mendenhall Glacier, which is only a few miles out of town, and is visited by thousands of tourists every summer. The city limits have been extended to include the Mendenhall, which brings its total area up to 3,108 square miles, of which 1,476 is land, 928 is ice cap, and 704 is water. Its population is just over 20,000.

I chose to see the glacier by rubber raft, combined with a four-hour float on the Mendenhall River from the lake at the foot of the glacier to a bridge close to the outlet. Our two five-man rafts made the trip without incident, although we all got pretty wet going through some heavy rapids. Didn't matter too much, as it was a rainy day anyway, and cold too, for this time of year. The raft owners supplied us with a lunch of smoked salmon, meats, cheese, crackers, and a combination warmer-upper which consisted of three parts champagne to one part peach brandy and one part apple cider. Good thing we were limited by the amount they provided!

Sightseeing in Juneau was interesting. Along with the interesting fact that one can walk out of second or third floors of buildings and be right on the side of the hill, there are many things of historical interest as well. The Governor's mansion, designed in Southern Colonial style, is a dominant feature of the mixed hillside buildings. Unlike many other Alaskan cities, Juneau has never suffered from flood, fire, or earthquake, so many of the landmarks remain. Of interest to gold mine buffs are the ruins of the Alaska-Juneau gold stamp mill, one of two deep shaft systems, the other being the Treadwell Mine on Douglas Island, which extended under the Gastineau Channel until it collapsed sometime prior to World War II.

There is an excellent museum, a fine library, good shops, and most of all, good people in Juneau. My brief stay was enjoyable.

Glacier Bay, my next stop, is only accessible by boat or plane, and going by 727 jet I arrived there in less than 15 minutes—the briefest flight I've ever had. I had a one-night reservation at Gustavus Inn, an old family-style farmhouse lodge which serves excellent food. They grow all their own vegetables. There is also Glacier Bay Lodge, which operates in conjunction with the National Park Service and is a much larger and more modern hotel and campground in the midst of a beautiful rain forest. It comes complete with a safe food cache for campers' groceries to prevent the bears from helping themselves.

In order to see the glaciers, it's necessary to take a boat trip that leaves at 6 a.m. and takes all day. So after an early rising call and a pancake and egg breakfast, we were off to the dock with just a hint of dawn approaching. The ship, the *Thunder Bay* (no relation to Ontario —so named because of the thundering of the glaciers), took about 50 aboard for the all-day cruise, accompanied by a naturalist from the Park Service who pointed out and explained things of interest. There are sixteen active glaciers within the park. The dark center lines indicate that they are composed of two or more contributory glaciers, as the line is debris that has accumulated along the sides of the smaller glaciers.

We were fortunate to see mountain goats from a distance, harbor seals, a few sea otters going through their fascinating eating and grooming procedures, and one humpback whale. Among the more unusual birds were oyster catchers, phalaropes, murrelets, scoters, and large black cormorants with their long necks, who perch on the taller trees looking quite omnipotent. I was sorry to hear that the puffins had already left for the winter. By lunch time the rains came, and only the hardiest (or the warmest and most appropriately dressed) of us ventured out on deck. Nearing Riggs Glacier we passed many icebergs, some a very brilliant turquoise, and of interesting shapes and sizes. The snow- and ice-clad mountains of the Fairweather Range are as impressive as the glaciers and are the source for all the glacial flow on this peninsula, which separates Glacier Bay from the Gulf of

*Portage Glacier.*

Alaska. The deep fiords are a direct result of glacial erosion caused by the ice mass moving forward over the underlying bedrock, widening and deepening the trough, and resulting in great landslides also. As the glaciers, which are composed of highly compressed ice and snow, recede, life quickly reinvades the land, which provides an unusual opportunity for botanists and biologists to observe what plants and animals are the first to grow from the apparently sterile soil.

In early afternoon we dropped off three girls who were going out for several days of backpacking, and would be picked up by whatever boat was going by at that time. We also off-loaded one fellow with his kayak and enough food for two weeks. I thought I recognized him, and after some conversation found out that he was one of the park naturalists at Denali Park who had spent some time with us there. That's apparently fairly typical of what Park employees do with their off time. It was a terrible day to start a venture, but I would gladly have joined one or the other if it had been possible.

The next day I spent hiking, enjoying the contrasts between the alpine tundra-like environment in one place, and the lush rain forest surrounding the lodge and the campground in another. Some of the big hemlocks must be three or four feet in diameter, and there is so much moss hanging from some that the shapes of the trees are lost, and they become strange caricatures. The village of Gustavus is about 10 miles from the lodge, and now boasts a grocery store as well as a church and a gift shop for the few families who winter over there. The Park employs only seven during the off season.

One night at the campground, which was too wet underfoot for reasonable tenting, was enough. I was glad I had purchased a pair of Southeast Sneakers, the rust-colored rubber boots that distinguish the local residents from the tourists. The following night the girl who was the Park Service naturalist on our boat invited me to share her trailer, which was a treat. I appreciated the chance to dry out my tent —it's heavy when wet. She, in turn, knew the girl I had stayed with in Nome, and the longer I stay here, the more I think Alaska is just one big small town after the tourists are removed. My friend Lois asked me to look up a ranger at Glacier Bay, and what happened? He was at Gustavus Inn for the family dinner the first night I was there.

Even with practically continuous rain it was a very pleasurable trip, and I won't forget it. After outfitting and making all the arrangements for a Camp Minocqua backpacking trip to Glacier Bay almost 10 years ago, it meant a lot to see it first hand. That trip was guided by Tuck and Peg Mallery of Minocqua and Wausau, Wisconsin, who did a lot to inspire me to come to Alaska. Unfortunately, I have to miss our friend, Bob Hertz, who is guiding a sheep hunt out of Cantwell in the Alaska Range. He left today to return, and I couldn't arrange to get to his fly-in cabin, in spite of a very cordial invitation.

A fine dinner in Juneau on our return from the glaciers with new friends from New York City, and one more night at the Alaska Hotel filled the time before a return ferry trip to Haines from Juneau. The M/V *Malaspina* coming north was not as full—only 125 passengers compared with 286 on the first trip. Vacationers are going home. The voyage to Haines takes only about five hours, traveling at about 12 knots per hour. These are truly luxury boats from every standpoint except the food, which is just average. They provide a good space for backpackers and foot travelers on the top floor in an open-ended enclosed area called the solarium, complete with deck chairs, indoor-outdoor carpeting, and some heat from radiant fixtures in the transparent fiberglass ceiling. It's a much more pleasant place to ride than in the enclosed, overheated lounges. As of October 1, I can ride the Alaska ferry free within the state during the off season. Another advantage of being over 65 years old.

Arriving in Haines in mid afternoon gave me time in the daylight to do more exploring around Port Chikoot, which was the original Fort William H. Seward, built in 1904. From 1897, when Alaska was purchased, until then, there had been no U.S. installation of any kind built in Alaska. Constructed in the same style as every other fort in the States at the time, it reflects the New England style of architecture. Each building rests on a firm foundation of hand-chiseled granite blocks. There are many buildings in the compound, which was purchased by a group of W.W.II veterans, who bought it surplus from the Army in 1947 for 105 million dollars. It was partially restored at that time, and has since been designated a historical site by both state and federal governments. Grants have been received to upgrade the property as well as provide for new buildings to house Tlingit Indian arts and programs, although these have been discontinued for the season.

The Halsingford Hotel occupies one of the remodeled buildings of the fort, and was the point of departure for the bus I took back to Anchorage. I forsook the comforts (and $) of the hotel, and pitched my tent across the street at the local campground.

Doing the return trip by bus all in the daylight was great. We did see the eagles just north of Haines, but only by the dozens instead of hundreds. The last spawning run of the Chum salmon in Alaska was going on in the Chilkoot River and its tributaries. The fish die, as you know, after spawning, so there is ample food for the eagles. And the temperate climate and open water keep them here all winter.

Sixty-five miles north of Haines we crossed the Chilkat Pass at about 3,500 feet, where they have reported 65 feet of snow and winds up to 200 m.p.h. These are beautiful snowcapped mountains, often reflected in alpine lakes. The aspen and birch are just turning color, which makes me realize that I have followed autumn colors south all the way from the Brooks Range in the past month. Later on, in magnificent Kluane (pronounced kloo-AAH-nee) Provincial Park in Yukon Territory, we saw 75 or 100 Dall sheep—where else, but on Sheep Mountain by Kluane Lake. This is a place to return to another year.

The bus follows the Wrangell Mountains after returning to Alaska, an extension of the St. Elias Mountains of Yukon Territory, and after turning at Glenallen, we bordered the Chugach Mountains to Anchorage. During a rest stop in Glenallen I called Gladys Bauers, who was about to leave for Woodruff, Wisconsin, and waved to her as we drove past her trailer home just out of town.

# CHAPTER 7

# Homer is
# Where the Heart Is

After a couple of days in Anchorage I decided to get on down to Homer, because many times since arriving in Alaska I've been asked "Have you been to Homer yet?" so I knew there was something special about it. Everyone seems to agree that it's one of the most beautiful places in the state. Homer is about 200 miles south of Anchorage on the Kenai Peninsula, and its spectacular location on Kachemak Bay, with the snow-covered Kenai Mountains as a background, makes it a favorite vacation area for Alaskans, as well as travelers from more faraway places.

*The mountains across Kachemak Bay from Homer.*

Fishing and tourism are the town's two industries, and the boat harbor is an interesting place to spend time, with its hundreds of fishing and recreational boats. Salmon and Dolly Varden trout are caught right off the beach on the spit, and commercial fishermen bring in thousands of pounds of halibut, crab, shrimp, and clams, as well as salmon.

Anchor Point, about fifteen miles north of Homer, is the most

*The Salty Dawg Saloon on Homer Spit.*

westerly place in North America that can be reached by road. It is an interesting fact when one looks at its location in the state to see that at approximately 152 degrees longitude, the entire two thirds of western Alaska has no road access. However, there are many small communities that are linked by a few miles of road systems, and some villages that have five or ten miles of roads (of a kind) that follow the old trails around town and to the airport. So one can see why the bush plane is really the only form of transportation for a large part of the state, along with the dog team and snowmobile, or boat, as the case may be.

The trip to Homer was interesting. During a conversation at the American Youth Hostel in Anchorage, after returning from Glacier Bay, someone mentioned a bargain air flight from there to the town of Kenai, which is about halfway to Homer, for only $20. I should explain that in order to go almost anywhere in southern Alaska, one must go through Anchorage. It was too good to pass up, so I made a reservation for that afternoon. When we were ready to take off, I discovered that there were only two of us aboard a plane that would seat about twenty. There are advantages to traveling at the end of the season, and the spectacular scenes only visible from the air made it a memorable trip. My fellow passenger, a masseur who teaches courses in various places around the state, was returning to Homer to conduct a class that evening. We had no trouble hitching the hundred miles from Kenai to Homer, and enjoyed the company of an old-time Soldotna fisherman who had many tales to tell of his experiences. We shared some of his exhilaration over his upcoming marriage to a beautiful Amazon-type young Army sergeant half his age, who seems to enjoy the prospect of being a deckhand.

One reason for going to Homer was to visit my friend Ed Berg, who drove me to Dawson to start my trip. He is from Madison, but is now suffering from a bad case of Alaska fever that causes otherwise sane people to wander off into the hills looking for available property to buy. He has been working as a carpenter here, summers only, for a number of years, and now plans to move up next spring.

When I called Ed to find out where I could find him that evening, he said, "Well, there's one complication. I have this massage class tonight..." As I was traveling with the instructor, there was no problem, and I then found myself enrolled in a class in Swedish massage. Good way to meet people. Ed's living arrangements and accommodations for a "guest" leave something to be desired, but I'm enjoying it immensely. The neighbors and the view easily make up for the lack of heat and water.

We're "camping" in an unfinished three-story home about ten miles out of town that overlooks the bay and the mountains. Ed built it several years ago for an older couple who changed their minds, and by blocking off a living area with plastic and using one small electric heater, we're finding it quite livable. Nights are below freezing and days alternate with sun and rain.

My days have been spent hiking up and down and around the surrounding mountains from the beach up to about 1,400 feet. The vistas are unbelievable. From the town and the road going northeast, which is were I'm staying, it's possible to see three glaciers coming down from the Kenai Icefields only about five miles away. Around on the southeasterly side of the Kenai peninsula are even more glaciers, including the famous Tustumena, which flows out of the Harding Icefield. If I can arrange it I'd like to take a sightseeing plane over the area.

Many of the names in this part of Alaska, both geographic and in the phone book, reflect the early Russian influence, and there are still Russian Orthodox churches to be seen in the villages.

I had an interesting visit with one of the early homesteaders of the area, Yule Kilcher, who lives almost directly down the hillside from us—a mile or so by trail. He acquired about 500 acres of what seems to me to be some of the finest land around. Certainly he has the most magnificent view! After raising a large family on his farm, he now lives alone in the original log cabin and rents another to a young

*View from the outhouse at Yule Kilcher's place.*

couple. Coming into his cabin is like stepping back in time about a hundred years, except for the telephone and electricity. The sweet smell of herbs drying in the rafters is almost lost to the strong odor of smoked salmon just brought in to the table. The two rooms reflect years of comfortable living and the strong personality of Yule, who seems as energetic approaching seventy as most of us were at forty. His planned job for the afternoon was to take his big tractor and trailer down to the beach to collect the last loads of coal for his winter heating and cooking. There is a vein of soft coal in the cliff a few miles northeast of Yule's place, from which large chunks drop to the beach; they can be picked up by anyone with the means to move them.

So off we went, Yule, his friend Fred, and I, bouncing almost out of the trailer as Yule apparently tried to show us how fast he could go careening downhill through the horse pasture, until a barbed wire gate slowed us down. Only temporarily. With renewed speed we sideslipped down a muddy canyon trail, through the alder brush slapping our faces, and finally out on the beach. If we thought that much was tough, beach travel was only a variation. Over rocks and driftwood and through still-wet sand which the big tires spat right up into our faces as we grabbed the sides of the trailer to keep from going out. Somehow it reminded me of a very rough rapids in a rubber raft, but much rougher and bumpier! It was interesting to watch the men standing on huge hunks of coal, swinging a pick to split off manageable chunks. I helped load up pieces I could handle, and after squeezing ourselves back into the trailer with the loaded coal, Yule couldn't get the tractor started. Only a click. The real problem was the tide. It would be devastating not to get the tractor out before the tide came in, so after the proper amount of tinkering and swearing by both men, we all hiked back to the farm—uphill for an hour or so—and they went back to the beach with another tractor to retrieve the first one. Successfully, thank goodness.

There were half a dozen kayaks stashed in the willows near the water, and after asking about them I learned that Yule cooperates with the National Outdoor Leadership School, and his place is a base for some of their kayaking and mountaineering programs in Alaska. That, combined with credit-earning students from Evergreen College in Olympia, Washington, where my daughter Ann graduated last year, keeps his place full of young people most of the time. We've been invited to come for a sauna, and plan to take him up on it.

Ed and I invited the young couple who live in a tiny cabin next door for dinner. He works with Ed, adding another floor and a tower to a house just a few hundred yards away, and she works at the radio station. They carry NPR programs here too, which is good, but the most interesting to me is the "Bush Line," which all radio stations in outlying areas of Alaska carry.

Another evening was spent at a poetry reading by a fairly well-known California writer, who followed up the next day with a workshop for writers and personal critiques. I enjoyed her reading and joined some new friends for the workshop the next day. There are many good things going on in this community, and with the end of the tourist season, people are greeting their neighbors again and beginning to relax after Homer's biggest tourist season ever. Other places of interest include the Pratt Museum, various workshops and gift shops where the local artists and artisans display their wares, and if one is interested, tours through the seafood plants can be arranged.

October—synonymous with snow in much of Alaska. With the first that has covered the ground, we hear it called "termination dust," as it terminates all summer activities. It will cause consternation to the cabin builders who haven't yet roofed in their buildings. Our friend next door works on the North Slope and says they've had snow for over a month, but Homer is in a temperate climate and it does seem early.

One day was spent digging potatoes (four varieties) for old-timer Yule Kilcher, followed by a potluck dinner, and a much-appreciated Finnish-style sauna, complete with a plunge in his homemade pool.

Another day we finally got around to taking down the large tipi that Ed and his family had lived in early in the summer. It was set up at the crest of the hill above Homer, with a view of the mountains across the bay, the coves and islands, and all of the town, from a height of about 1,600 feet.

On a clear day it's possible to see the symmetrical cone of Augustine Volcano rising up in Cook Inlet. The most active in south central Alaska, it last blew its top in 1976, spreading ash over much of the Cook Inlet region. It also erupted twice in the '60s, and four times previous to that, according to the records. Two other volcanoes in the area are Redoubt at 10,000 feet, 50 miles west of Kenai, which erupted three times in the '60s, as well as earlier. Iliamna is the third, located south of Redoubt, and about the same height. It hasn't erupted in this century.

Last evening some friends came for dinner and brought sliced cold octopus for an appetizer, to be eaten with a sharp mustard or lime juice. It was better than any I had tasted before, no doubt because it had been swimming around the bay the day before. In terms of marine life, Kachemak Bay is one of the richest bodies of water in Alaska, and I have been treated to a good sampling of its many varieties over the past few weeks. In a few days I'll be having fresh clams, thanks to a couple recently moved here from New Hampshire, who picked me up when I needed a ride from town. They sent a message via the "Bay Bush Line." Quite a surprise to hear my name over the local radio.

I'm finding more and more people, mostly in their 30s or 40s, who have moved to Alaska recently and have simplified their lifestyles to eliminate many of the energy-consuming frills of modern civilization. It's an encouraging trend. Their reasons for coming are many and varied, but they seen to share a similar sense of values.

Early in the week Ed Berg and I enjoyed a visit with Debbie and Roy Smith, friends of Bob Hertz who lives in Lac du Flambeau, Wisconsin. Roy is another fine carpenter—he has a large shop that would be the envy of any craftsman, and his two-story log home is full of fine detail work, as well as furniture that he has constructed. They live high on the ridge above town with their young daughter, and it's good that the winters aren't too severe here or no one would make it up and down the hills.

# HOMER IS WHERE THE HEART IS

Interesting people pick me up going to and from town when I go —old settlers who wish the town would stay as it was many years ago; young people who have just moved here and think they've found their Shangri-La; fishermen who would prefer to be on the water; women going shopping; and the usual number of young people most interested in speeding around in their four-wheel-drive trucks.

Yesterday an older man told me about a woman who some years ago was the owner of the only grocery store in town. A true eccentric, she would only sell fresh vegetables to people she approved of. If she really didn't like a person, she wouldn't sell them any groceries at all, making it almost impossible for her victims to continue living in town.

Similar to other small towns, there are many dogs here, but few seem to run the streets. In Alaska, generally, most dogs fall into one of two categories. One includes all the sled dogs, which are born and raised to work. Their lives consist of sledding in the winter, and very little activity during the remainder of the year. Most live in the interior or northern sections of Alaska. They are always chained, and spend a lot of their time sitting on top of their dog houses barking and howling. The other type ride around in the back of pickup trucks (universal Alaskan vehicle), barking at anything of interest in passing, but never getting out of the truck, no matter how long it is parked away from home. Sometimes there are three or four dogs in one truck.

For several days I visited Jan and Ed Schofield, the couple who gave me a lift from town previously. Just the process of getting to their house is an adventure in itself. First, a drive out of town about 15 or 20 miles to the end of a dirt road, park the car, then proceed along a mud road that makes even walking a risk. Shortly that becomes a path that winds through and around a few farms perched high up on a plateau. By this time of year the hay is in and the cattle have been herded down to lower pastures on the bay. One farmer we met was just packing up to go south for the winter. The trail descended from there downhill through moss-draped spruce and big cottonwood trees, along the edge of Swift Creek canyon. The only

*Jan and Ed Schofield.*

remaining green foliage is the gigantic-leaved devil's club, so named because the heavy stems are covered with spines that resemble cactus. Not something I'd wish to fall into.

We arrived after a few miles at David's Place, which is an area consisting of a storage shed, frame for a small barn, one tent, an outhouse with a view, the beginning of a log cabin, a small pasture, and lots of garden. Obviously, he would prefer gardening to cabin building, as the house has been in the process for several years. He has his eyes on a nearby empty cabin for the winter.

The trail from David's drops over the edge of the cliff, and in some places seems safer to back down. I found out later that there is an alternative switchback route that is considerably longer, and vowed that given my choice, I would come back up that way! The panoramic views along the way were lovely, and at one spot we had a clear view of a new Old Russian community that is nestled into the Swift Creek valley along the shore of Kachemak Bay. Eventually we made it all the way down, to find an old log cabin with a shiny new stovepipe hugging the lower grassy slope not far above the high-tide mark. There were two outbuildings in disrepair, one usable as a chicken coop and the other a stable and tack shed for the two horses which were frequent guests.

Jan and Ed are renting for the winter, and are cabin building across the bay about six miles out of the isolated fishing village of Seldovia. No roads in, as it is surrounded by impassable mountains, as are most Alaskan fishing villages. Ed built log houses in New Hampshire before coming here, so has had plenty of experience. They added a barrel stove to the wood range in the cabin, so that, combined with a double-layer down comforter, should keep them warm this winter. It's an attractive, cozy place to live, with the usual spectacular view of the mountains across the bay.

Highlights of the two-day visit were horseback riding along the beach, digging fresh clams with David and eating them for breakfast, tasting his birch syrup—a first for me, hiking up Swift Creek to visit some unusual old log buildings, and then coming back through the new Russian settlement.

The Russian influence in this part of Alaska proves to be more than just place names and remains of old churches. After seeing both men and women in the Homer stores dressed in the traditional Russian garb, I inquired and found that they come from a village just northwest of here, near Anchor Point, called Nikolaevsk. The town was founded about 15 years ago by expatriate Russian "Old Believers," whose ancestors refused to accept reforms in the rites of the Russian Orthodoxy in 1950.

They rely primarily on fishing, construction work, and boat building for their livelihood. Their clothing is colorful; the women wearing long, pinafore-type dresses and bright peasant head scarves, and the men wearing boots and high-necked embroidered shirts. Although they are cordial to talk with, they are not altogether enthusiastic about having tourists in their village.

Ed was interested in buying a door from one of the old cabins, so we had a reason to visit there. It's well known that they don't welcome visitors, so at least we had an excuse. I would like to have taken pictures of some of the old men, but hesitated to ask them— many speak no English. I did photograph a younger man leading several horses, however, on the pretext of taking a picture of a colt that was with him.

The Russians build their own boats, which are very colorful and provide their source of income, but their houses are strictly un-imaginative square American boxes. Very efficient, I'm sure. Small children at the windows watching us neither smile nor wave, and the women disappear the moment they see us. Truly a secluded and closed-in culture.

The girls' fiancees are selected by the fathers, and they are married at 14 or 15 regardless of their own preferences. Some look like children themselves with one or two babies tagging along, all dressed in Russian peasant style. It's hard to believe that there are still such communities in the U.S.

When it came time to leave Swift Creek, Dave, who is taking care of the two horses, wanted them brought up to the pasture at his place because the Schofields were coming out with me for a couple of days. Riding a big stallion up the switchback trail with a pack (fairly light) was another new experience for me. It was slick mud in spots, and the horses had some trouble with their footing, which was especially hairy when we were close to the edge of the canyon. But thankfully, the horses were more accustomed to the trail than I was, and their sure-footed instincts took over.

We had extra time around town, the weather was clear and bright for the first time in a week, so we decided to take a float plane up to see the Homer area from the air. Ed and Jan were delighted to see the valley where they are building, and I was amazed at the magnificent views in the mountain tops. There are more bays, islands. and coves than I had imagined.

One evening we attended a concert by one of the Kilcher boys, his wife, three children, and a friend. They live in Anchorage and perform and record regularly there, doing homegrown-type Alaskan songs, many original. There was a large turnout for it. We were invited for a dinner before the concert at another Kilcher's home, (Yule, the homesteader, raised eight children in his two-room log cabin), and quite a few people returned there after the performance, along with the stars of the evening, for a good party.

Another happy coincidence: two girls I met at the party are working in Anchorage doing research in the villages for the Bureau of Indian Affairs, and came to my rescue with names of people to see, villages to visit, and how to get to them when I arrive on Kodiak Island in a few days. To date I had only known one young man from the Park Service whom I met in Kotzebue, who lives there and offered floor space for my sleeping bag.

# CHAPTER 8

# Odyssey
# to the
# Aleutians

# SOLO ON THE YUKON

AFTER A BEAUTIFUL FAREWELL PARTY, I RELUCTANTLY SAID GOODBYE TO MY Homer friends, with promises to return. My next visit is Kodiak Island, by way of Alaska Ferry. It's an overnight trip, and I will be there for a week, which will give me enough time to fly out to some of the villages and do some sightseeing. The ferry is the *Tustumena,* but is affectionately called the *Rusty Tusty,* or some such name. It's the only truly ocean-going ferry in the fleet, and from what I hear of this trip, which will continue on out the Aleutian chain to Dutch Harbor, it is always a very rough and difficult one, particularly at this time of year.

*The Alaska Ferry* Tustumena *ready to embark.*

There is no such thing as a schedule for this trip, which traditionally is only taken twice a year, but this is the fourth, and last, for 1981. The captain merely blasts his horn long enough for everyone to hear, even in a sound sleep, to announce his arrival along the way. Sometimes they are a day or two behind schedule.

The M/V *Tustumena* has been in service for 18 years, and due to the fact that construction money ran out before the ship was completed, it was originally 85 feet shorter than its planned design. Needless to say, this affected the vessel's stability, so after several years of rocking and rolling, she was hauled out and 56 feet of staterooms and engine space were added, making her a more gentle and graceful ship. She accommodates 220 passengers and a crew of 40.

Many of the crew have been with the ship for 10 or 15 years, and in contrast to the other ferries that have two full crews alternating all the time, the *Tusty* crew works for two to three months before taking their six-week vacation break. Home base is Seward, and although the lifestyle can be hard on families, it's an excellent job according to its members, who appreciate the good pay, the benefits, and the family atmosphere. All this, of course, is reflected in their attitude toward the passengers, and should result in a delightful experience for anyone aboard.

It may prove otherwise on the Dutch Harbor run, as the *Tustumena* has probably been responsible for more near-fatal cases of seasickness than any other Alaskan state ferry. The National Geographic nicknamed her the *Dramamine Express* in a 1975 issue of the magazine. They say her course takes her into some of the roughest water and worst weather in the world, along the Aleutian Chain.

Unexpectedly, the overnight ferry trip from Homer to Kodiak was quite smooth, except for a little rolling in the middle of the night. A full moon came out shortly after leaving, and shone brightly all night, to the great joy of many of the passengers who stayed up quite late to enjoy it. I met three members of the regular crew who were on vacation, riding "their" ferry to Port Lions on Kodiak Island to hunt Sitka blacktail deer.

After a few beers one of them suggested that he take me up to the bridge to meet the captain and observe the navigation. What a fine opportunity that was! He introduced me to the captain and then disappeared—to bed, no doubt, as the group had to disembark at 5 a.m. Captain Hofstad, who was born in Petersburg, Alaska, and has been a seagoing man all his life, has been with the *Tustumena* for 17 years. He is a very cordial person, and I look forward to seeing more of him when I reboard the ship after my week's visit in Kodiak.

The bridge is a fascinating place to be, especially at night, and even more especially with a full moon casting a luminous glow over all the instruments and the wheel. Only the instruments are lighted, so that outside visibility is improved, and being so far from the motor and the passengers, there are no sounds to disturb the softness of the night except brief instructions from captain to crew where necessary. Rather an eerie atmosphere.

My contact in Kodiak was a young man, Bud Rice, from the Park Service, whom I met in Kotzebue earlier in my trip. He is now teaching in the high school, has extra space in his house, and coincidentally, rents a room to a girl who is leaving the FM radio station here to move to Homer and join the staff of their station. She was interviewed by, and will work with a girl who lived next door to where I stayed in Homer. Small world.

Some notes about Kodiak. The island is the second largest under the U.S. flag, with Hawaii, of course, being the largest. About two thirds of it is a National Wildlife Refuge—home of the famous Kodiak brown bear, the small Sitka blacktail deer, and many other species. It occupies an area more than twice the size of Rhode Island, and I've had some opportunity to do a little hiking in it.

The town of Kodiak, similar to most south central and southeast towns, is spread out along the shore and around the harbor, with hills and mountains rising up behind. The island has been inhabited for almost 6,000 years, the majority of the time by people of the Eskimo tradition.

The Russians, in their search for furs, first encountered the Kodiak Natives in 1762, and in 1784 the first white settlement was established. The Russian Orthodox Church of the Holy Resurrection was built in 1774 and was the first Christian Church to be introduced into Russian America. It was rebuilt in recent times, following a fire, and contains the holy relics of St. Herman of Alaska, who is the only saint of the Orthodox Church in this hemisphere. Many miracles have been attributed to him, and he was canonized here in 1970.

It was my pleasure to attend the Saturday evening service there. The interior was aglow with the lights of more than a hundred candles reflected in the elaborate brass holders and the large crystal chandelier. Both the exterior, with its bright blue onion domes, and the interior are faithful reproductions of the original church. Most of the service was in English but some was in Aleut, and I believe some in Russian. The music was beautiful.

In 1912, Mount Katmai, a hundred miles away on the mainland, erupted, covering Kodiak with 18 inches of volcanic ash, which can still be found under the topsoil of the area. It is now Katmai National Park, which contains the Valley of Ten Thousand Smokes. In 1964 the earthquake and tidal wave that did so much damage to this part of Alaska virtually wiped out the downtown area of Kodiak. It has been redesigned and rebuilt, so it no longer resembles a quaint old fishing village but an up-to-date modern city.

Many of Kodiak's 5,000 people are employed in the fishing industry in one way or another. The port is consistently among the top three in the U.S. in the value of fish and shellfish landed, and is home port for one of the largest fishing fleets in the U.S. There are very few pleasure boats, and the fishing boats run from 20 feet to around 100 feet in length, and from old lapstrake rusted-out, patched-together hulls, to the newest in stainless steel.

Some have permanent occupants, well covered with plastic for the winter, but most are cleaned up and battened down to wait for spring. The truly hardy members of the fleet are the ones who fish all winter. Crab and shrimp are coming in now and the canneries operating, but not at full capacity.

I had a sneak-in view of a king crab plant, one of about twenty processing plants in Kodiak, and decided that would be on the bottom of my list of possible jobs.

I'm being spoiled again as far as meals are concerned. First night here I treated—fresh halibut. The next night Bud and the girls fixed up a filet of blacktail venison that was so tender it could be cut with a fork. And the last night someone gave us fresh king crab.

*Kodiak harbor's fishing fleet.*

Always wanting to visit the smaller villages, I made arrangements to fly by mail plane to the village of Ouzinkie on nearby Spruce Island. It almost resulted in my missing the *Tustumena* on her way out of the Aleutians.

What happened? Well, a couple of typical days for this time of year closed in, and no one would fly or boat me out of the village of Ouzinkie, where I had been visiting for a few days. The town is on Spruce Island, just north of Kodiak Island. Rain and high winds kept the mail plane from coming in on Tuesday, which was the day I would have had to leave if the ferry was on time. All I could do was wait it out—and hope.

A good lady named Fran invited me to her cabin on the other side of the bay, an hour's walk from the village. It was a fairy land of oversize spruce trees hung with moss, giving a ghostly appearance to the forest. Fran lives alone with three cats and a dog in a 14- by 16-

foot cabin that looks as if it had grown there. Her job with the village is teaching adults and giving GED tests.

Fortunately, she had a CB radio. It was turned on early in the morning to hear anything that might be going on, and we found that the weather was clearing, that the *Tustumena* was running half an hour late and, of course, all kinds of personal messages were going back and forth. By relaying a message we were able to arrange a charter plane to come out and take me in to Kodiak. Boarding and coming ashore from these small float planes is an interesting process. The pilot picks up his passengers on the beach and carries them piggyback to the plane, or off the plane. Fortunately for him, I was wearing my Southeast Sneakers (translate rubber boots), but I wonder how he'd make it with really heavy people.

No problem getting to the ferry on time, although I did a lot of running in the process. Because this was a "first," there were a good number of passengers.

Back to Ouzinkie: Set in a picturesque cove of Spruce Island, it is a typical small (population 180) fishing village, predominantly Aleut. New homes are being built there, and a new road system is being constructed that will be about ten miles long. A well-kept Russian church overlooks the bay, the post office is a tiny frame building connected to a boardwalk that goes from the general store to some of the older homes on a high bank above the water. There is also a Baptist Mission there, that had been suggested to me as a possible place to stay. Reverend Smith has retired from the ministry, but his wife continues to operate a nursery school and a preschool class every day. She is also the only available medical help on the island.

Another classic: Joyce Smith turned out to be the cousin of my friend Celia Hunter from Fairbanks. We had a good visit between interruptions, and I enjoyed three days with them in the big old mission building that was a boarding school at one time. Reverend Smith, although retired, is probably the busiest man in the village, as he operates the town generator (all lights go out at 10 p.m.), picks up and delivers mail between the post office and the mail plane, and monitors and handles all emergency calls on the CB. He is one person everyone in the village knows can be relied on.

The first day I was there I had the privilege of meeting two of the town's elder women. They are remarkable. Both are in their upper 80s and are active, spry, and very full of pep and sharp wit. Both were born and raised in Ouzinkie and have been friends all their lives.

Sasha, the elder, took Fran and me for a walk, which I thought would be around on the new roads, but no, off we went through the woods for about two miles, ending at the town dump. She had many stories to tell of the old days, but her friend Jenny's bear stories were most exciting. She told of a Kodiak bear, about nine feet tall, coming into her garden and then attempting to get into her house, all of which happened only a few years ago.

The women were having a potluck luncheon the day I left, and some were hopeful that I would be able to stay over for it. They were serving edible wild foods, and I would have enjoyed it, but couldn't stay.

Until the past few weeks I hadn't realized how many people in this part of Alaska are of Russian lineage. The place names I knew, but it was a surprise to find so many Russian names in the telephone directories or on the school rosters.

So, following a week ashore, I again boarded the M/V *Tustumena* to continue my sea voyage. Captain Hofstad has worked for years to persuade the Alaska Department of Transportation that this route should be put on the regular schedule. He is hopeful that this trip will prove his point. The capacity of the *Tusty* is 200 passengers and about 40 crew members. There are 25 two-berth staterooms, and a car deck that holds 54 cars. She is the only ship in the world which can load and unload vehicles at any dock at any tide stage without a loading ramp. More details: the *Tustumena* was built in Sturgeon Bay in 1964, remodeled in 1969 and made more seaworthy by the addition of fin stabilizers. New bow thrusters enable the ship to move sideways for docking and departing.

This makes it sound as if there could be no problem in high seas, but we've all figured out that what we really need is a horizon stabilizer! Every so often the captain gets on the loud speaker to remind the passengers to hang onto the handrails when moving about. He also keeps us posted regarding arrival and departure times, which change from day to day. But what we like to hear most is "whales blowing—20 degrees off the starboard bow!" or such information. So far we've seen one large grey whale, four orcas, and any number of porpoise.

There are all types and varieties of people on board. A senior citizen group from Anchorage, with ages up to 80 or more. A basketball team from Port Lyon, which ferried overnight to play at Sand Point (and won). Young people leaving their cannery jobs to return to the lower 48 for the winter. An elderly Aleut gentleman, impeccably dressed, traveling alone and for the first time, going out the Aleutian chain. The bartender, in his fourth year on the *Tusty,* is a mild-mannered graduate of Dartmouth College, who nonetheless seems able to cope with the problems of over-imbibing patrons. Unlike the large ferries, the *Tustumena* has only a six-stool bar in the corner of the dining room, which is only open from 11 a.m. to 2 p.m., and from 5 to 10 p.m.

The Chief Steward has been with the ship for many years, and has mastered the art of carrying dishes, taking orders, and at the same time, weaving his way around the stationery tables and seats with great alacrity. Luckily we have rims around the edges of the tables, but even so, there were any number of crashes in the kitchen when stacks of china fell to the floor and rolled around.

There are several Aleutian families "going out" to visit friends or relatives, or to work, and one couple with all their worldly possessions and a baby, moving to Kodiak. Conversations on board cover many extremes from philosophy to fishing, and from religion to hunting.

Floor sleeping in the enclosed-on-three-sides solarium is very pleasant. The weather has been quite mild, although some nights brought a fine spray of mist (rain?) in under the roof, and the rolling often causes entire sleeping systems (body included) to move magically from one space to another. An average of about 20 people use this area.

Brief landings at the villages have been interesting. Most of the views from the ship are open sea on one side and bare islands on the other, stretching out as far as we can see. The Aleutian Peninsula extends to about 163 degrees longitude, where Unimak Island begins the series of volcanic isles that extend more than a thousand miles west and south, ending at Attu Island. Attu is well known because of the Japanese invasion there during World War II. The Aleutian Mountains extend the full length of the peninsula and down the islands to form the Ring of Fire. Many are volcanic, and of the six that we are able to see from the boat, one has been active in quite recent years. Others are almost bare rock. There are no trees on the islands except where they have been planted. The ones at Dutch Harbor were planted by the Russians 150 years ago, and are just now beginning to reproduce themselves.

Interesting notes along the way: Sand Point boasts a population of about 900 people, which soars during the summer to 1,500

*View of Dutch Harbor from the boat.*

*Russian Orthodox church in Dutch Harbor.*

because of the fishing operations. The community seems to have a large number of new cars, considering the few miles of road available, and judging from the number of abandoned wrecks, they seldom repair a vehicle, but merely order a new one. Sand Point is second only to Valdez in wealth per capita in Alaska.

Cold Bay is just what its name implies. Within sight of Shisbalden volcano, the largest in the chain, it is another small fishing village, as is King Cove. Our arrival time in Dutch Harbor was delayed because of high winds, and we came in at 11:30 p.m., a bit late to take the three-mile hike into town, although a few intrepid souls did go, only to find everything closed up.

Because the captain had wanted to take this run for a long time, he arranged to have an open house, which had to be done in the morning. While the townspeople were welcomed aboard, we took a school bus to town to visit all we could in the hour available to us. Unalaska and Dutch Harbor are twin towns, with an extensive harbor system. Dutch Harbor is the site of an extensive World War II military installation, and has the largest supply of scrap iron I've ever seen. Remains of quonset huts, battlements, bunkers, old trucks, and a small mountain of rusted-out double-decker bunks and springs are scattered around the hillsides—empty reminders of a long-gone era when thousands of servicemen were stationed there. Added to the historical interest surrounding Dutch Harbor is also the fact that it is the biggest money-making fishery in America per capita, bar none.

The return trip was quieter than our outbound voyage. The sun came out and we were able to see things that we missed before. We were treated to a movie, *Mr. Roberts,* a real oldie, but a good one.

Of some 200 islands in the Aleutian Chain, only six have villages, and they certainly qualify as the most isolated and remote settlements in America. There are numerous stories that have come down through the years relating to shipwrecks, plane wrecks, or just stories of survival in a hostile environment. An ingenious example was when a boat ran out of motor oil, so the captain and a crew member killed a seal, rendered its oil, and used it in place of motor oil. It worked. When asked by a young pilot stranded at Atka, "Say, when does your season change up here? When does winter end and spring begin?" the answer was, "Don't be funny. We have only two seasons, this winter and next winter."

A word or two about our capable captain, Richard Hofstad: He is a quiet, dignified man who has always been a seaman. Born and raised in Petersburg, he first joined his father in commercial fishing when he was six years old. He fished salmon with his uncle in 1949 when they thought 50 cents was a good price for a fish. He joined the Merchant Marine during World War II and was drafted into service again for the Korean War. He traveled the world with the Merchant Marine, but always missed Petersburg, so when he learned in 1962 that Alaska was starting a state ferry system, he joined the company. He worked up the ladder from seaman to pilot to chief's mate to skipper in the next five years, and his first assignment was aboard the *Chikat* on Prince William Sound in 1968.

This entire trip has been fascinating from the first day to the last.

There is a very special magic about the Aleutians, and I'm sorry not to be able to spend more time here. It's a strange and beautiful place.

Our final destination was Seward, at the tip of the Kenai Peninsula. The last leg of the journey was overnight, so we didn't see much of the beautiful glaciated peaks of the Kenai Mountains and the large Harding Icefield.

Our arrival at first light in the morning revealed lovely views from the slip and a busy scene on the wharf, as this was the end of the ferry trip and also the southern terminus of the Alaska railroad. There were many vehicles to be offloaded, as well as people meeting passengers.

After some heart-felt goodbyes to the crew, some other guests, and especially to the group of about 30 senior citizens from Anchorage who had been such good sports, I was relieved to be offered a ride back to Anchorage by a woman who is a reporter for the *Anchorage Daily News,* even though it was 200 miles in the back of a pickup (with topper).

# CHAPTER 9

# Dog Sled
# and
# Down Home

# SOLO ON THE YUKON

IT TOOK A DAY OR SO FOR ME TO GET MY LAND LEGS BACK, AND I ENJOYED relaxing with Flo Mason, who was the program director for the senior citizen group, and had made the arrangements for the trip. She lives in a lovely home overlooking Cook Inlet. There were interesting things to see and do, among them a trip to the University with enough time at the library to browse through a fine collection of Alaskana, a night at the opera, a lunch at the senior center, and much more. The opera was *Die Fledermaus,* and I'm sure that Alaska is the only place where one can attend dressed as I was in wool pants, hiking boots, and down jacket, and not feel out of place.

After several days of city life (and one day of housecleaning for my hostess) I decided to move along and return to Fairbanks, where Celia Hunter and Ginny Wood have made me think of their house as my home away from home. The word that the Alaska Railway only runs one train a week during the winter made up my mind for me, as another week in the big city of Anchorage might have been enough to destroy my good feelings about it. The 9-to-5 rat race is thriving in Anchorage.

My earlier trip on the Alaska Railroad was with friends, going from McKinley Park to Anchorage in September—in reverse direction, so much of the beautiful part of the trip was in the dark. It's an all-day trip to Fairbanks, and although some of the old-time charm has gone (Ginny tells of the winter train stopping long enough for the crew to get off to cut wood for an ailing homesteader who lived alone somewhere along the tracks), the stove in the diner is an old wood range, and the engineer stops for anyone who flags down the train.

It being Halloween, passengers were greeted by the dining car being completely decorated to celebrate the occasion and the waiters wearing outlandish costumes. Halloween seems to be much more of an occasion in Alaska than anywhere else. Perhaps with the shorter days, any old excuse for a party is worthwhile, but I don't ever recall seeing any bank tellers and business people in costume all day at work. Great fun!

So it didn't surprise me too much when Celia met me at the

station and chauffeured me off to a large party where everyone was in costume. This was an annual affair that originated some 25 years ago when these outlying families had small children and it was impossible to get them to town for "tricks and treats." They are all grown now and the numbers have increased, so it's a two-generation potluck party for about 50 people—all attired in very clever homemade costumes.

Many people had warned me, but even so I wasn't prepared for the cold in Fairbanks—zero this morning, the first of November. After the relatively moderate climate in Kodiak and the Aleutians, which of course are warmed by the Japanese Current, it's hard to believe such a change in only five or six hundred miles. Anchorage, 400 miles south, has had only a sprinkling of snow and not much cold weather. Fairbanks has a fair snow cover, almost enough to ski!

Worth passing on as a fact of life in not-so-rural Alaska, is the news that Celia's and Ginny's garden was invaded three times by moose since I was here last. Once it was a cow and calf, showing definite preference for cabbage, broccoli, and peas, after pushing over a six-foot fence. Another took a liking to a patch of kale, and by the time a third raid occurred, I think a decision was made to protect all the gardens with the same heavy double fence that they have erected around the one untouched area. Or perhaps the moose can read, and all that is needed is more signs like the one hanging there that says, "Fort Vamoose."

It wasn't long before I began to have more frequent thoughts of home and family, and it became apparent that the right time to return would be sooner than the "I'll be back for Christmas" that I had said all along. The original plan was to stay for Thanksgiving to see Mary Shields and John Manthei again, enjoy dogsledding with them, and then come home slowly via the White Pass and Yukon narrow-gauge railroad and the Alaska ferry to Seattle with stops in Sitka, Petersburg, and other southeastern towns. But long before this time I knew that I would be returning to Alaska another year ('83 or '84?) and didn't need to attempt the impossible by trying to see even all four corners of the state in one season. So with that thought I was willing to save the dogsledding until later, along with my planned visits to Southeast Alaska.

The next step was to call my Minocqua family, Dare and Mary, and then make plane reservations. This done, I sat back to enjoy the last few days with my good friends, Celia and Ginny, when a phone call came for me from John Manthei.

John had come in by dogsled to his summer cabin near Fairbanks for a few days to pick up supplies to haul back out to Schimmel-pfennig, which is the name of the winter cabin that he shares with Mary, as well as the name of the creek that provides their water. When he heard that I was planning to leave in a few days, he invited me to go back with him the following morning and promised to get me back for the plane late Saturday night. No need to give up the dogsledding. And what a treat it was!

After picking me up we drove out to John's shop, where the dogs were staked out and a friend was waiting to ride out to the start of the trail in order to bring the truck back. The dogs were so excited that they almost jumped out of their skins before they leaped into the loaded truck and were each snapped onto a short chain attached to the sides of the truck.

It was 15 or 20 miles to where Mary was waiting for us with her team. She reported that the trail was icy, but the temperature was in the 20s, so it was a good day, and it didn't take long to load every-thing into the open tarp, fold it over and tie it securely. This is essential, as the sled can easily overturn, even with a skilled driver.

Sled dogs are amazing animals. Throughout history the Natives of the Arctic and subarctic regions have used dogs to transport goods from one hunting ground to another, as well as to track and harass the polar bear, sniff out seals beneath the ice, and be useful in may other ways. Little is known of their use in prehistoric times, but there is evidence that dogs accompanied early people across the Bering Land Bridge as they moved from Siberia to Alaska. As these people became isolated from one another, the dogs developed geographically distinct characteristics which can be seen in the present-day breeds. Most teams are composed of mixed breeds, although some people prefer to

*Mary and John, each with their own dog team,
and two pups who are "in training."*

have a matched team for show purposes. The dominant breeds are Greenland Eskimo, Siberian Husky, and Alaskan Malamute, although many sled dogs are part Labrador, part Shepherd, or part mutt. The Samoyed is also trained as a sled dog.

These dogs are eager to run, have learned to cope with many dangerous situations, and can survive in the coldest weather because of their double coat of fur and their ability to lie curled up tightly in a ball with their nose and pads protected under a bushy tail.

The lead dog is most important, of course, as his immediate response to commands could be a matter of life and death, and he must set the pace for the team. The best leaders develop a wariness for thin ice and other dangers on the trail and are not diverted by any other animals nearby. Both John and Mary are using teams of seven dogs each. One of their females had pups last spring, and two were kept as replacements to be trained for future work, one for Mary's old lead dog, Cabbage, who is now in her teens. That's elderly for a sled dog, as most prefer to be retired at 8 or 10. She kept up all right but not as lead dog. The pups are half grown and accompanied us all the way, trying very hard to impress us (and their mother) with their endurance and enthusiasm. They are anxious to become working members of their community, and it's often hilarious to see them trying to act like self-controlled adult dogs while they're tripping over their own big feet.

At home, each dog is on a chain that reaches far enough for them to sit on top of their log house, be in it, or run around the stake, but that isn't long enough to reach another dog. The puppies, however, have the run of the area and are allowed in the house as well.

What was most impressive to me was the apparent ease with which the team travels once under way, and the quickness with which they respond to Mary's soft-spoken commands. I was traveling with her and taking the driver's position when the going was fairly smooth and there were no rivers to cross or banks to fall down. Once when we were stopped I answered her question with an "O.K.," which she had forgotten to tell me was the dogs' signal to start, so they immediately took off, leaving me in the snow and Mary barely hanging on.

The three-hour sled run seemed more like one, and before long we were approaching a large stand of the tallest spruce trees I had seen in central Alaska. First the dog houses came in view, then up the hill the cabin nestled into the ground and I could see that it had the traditional sod roof. Close by stood the ever-present cache—the only way to store food in the bush, as a grizzly is capable of forcing himself into almost any cabin if he really wants to. John built his (a miniature log cabin on a platform, also with a sod roof), with a very long ladder to reach it, and the bottom third of the log supports covered with tin to keep the climbing predators away. His skills as a carpenter and cabinet maker come out in every building, and combined with the eye of an artist, the entire place has an aura of beauty about it. A wood shed and lumber storage area are

*Mary and John's winter cabin, with the sauna in the foreground.*

combined; a large workshop provides plenty of space, and an attractive sauna is part way down the hill toward the creek. The almost typical bush Alaskan outhouse—no door, large overhang for rain and snow protection, and always a beautiful view—completes the scene.

I continue to be spoiled by my friends as far as food is concerned: moose stew, moose roast, smoked salmon (like candy), and all kinds of goodies including homegrown vegetables from their summer cabin garden made me marvel at the quality of John and Mary's food. They have a radio, and listen every night to Trapline Chatter, but have no way of getting in touch with the outside world except by dogsled, and it's a long way in to Fairbanks!

Cooking up the food for the dogs is a big job almost every day, and the statistics of it are impressive. The diet is supplemented by rabbits, which are plentiful, and Mary has learned to snare and cut up the four a day that are added to the stew, skin and all—after she removes the stomachs for study by Alaska Fish and Game Department. Here is what is needed for two teams working from October through April: 900 pounds cornmeal, 1,100 pounds salmon (whole), 560 pounds meat and fish meal, 1,600 pounds Purina chow, 800 pounds fat. If you figure dog chow alone, one 50 pound bag would last three days!

It was a great treat to join John and Mary for a sauna, which was almost too hot for me, though I managed by staying in the corner away from the stove. A little snow on the body afterward felt good, and a full moon through the trees gave a dream-like quality to the whole experience and seemed a most appropriate way to conclude my visit, not only with Mary and John but with all of Alaska and my friends there.

We were up at five the next morning, and I was again reminded of an important reason for not living close to town with a dog team. They not only "sing" occasionally at night, but the moment someone moves out of doors they think they are going to either be fed or hooked up to the sled, and can scarcely stop barking in anticipation. It was still almost dark when we got going, and as the sky grew gradually lighter we were able to see the delicate beauty of the frost on every twig and branch and feel the fresh new snow on our faces as we whisked silently along. Unforgettable.

Before going to Schimmelpfennig, I had been invited to dinner with Carol and Jim, who were the leaders of the August Brooks Range backpacking trip. It was good to see them again, and following that I had lunch with Susan, who had joined us on one of the ferry boat trips. Departing that same night on the Red Eye Special (aptly named, Northwest Orient Airlines, Fairbanks to Seattle, leaving at midnight) was interesting. I had said goodbye to Celia earlier as she was at a meeting in Anchorage, and Ginny joined Carol and Jim to see me off. My backpack was light, but my old canoeing pack which had been stored all summer was just the thing to bring back the large quantities of moose meat and salmon from John and Mary, to be delivered to Sue (John's sister) and Dave Pucci, Sue and John's parents, and also some for Mary's mother and some for me, too. Wrapped well, it was still frozen when I arrived in Minocqua 15 hours and only a catnap later.

My thanks to all the people along the way who in many ways *were* the trip. Their help and friendship made it all work.

And thanks to the *Lakeland Times* staff, who had to decipher these notes that came in sporadically from some pretty strange places. They did a fine job.

# FACTS ABOUT ALASKA

**DID YOU KNOW...**

Alaska has the greatest number of pilots and light aircraft in the United States: six times as many pilots per capita and twelve times as many airplanes per capita as compared to the rest of the U.S.

The blanket toss is not a game, but a system of sighting whales. The Eskimos used to choose the person with the best eyesight and they would toss him high enough to spot whales out at sea.

The word *cheechako,* used by old-time Alaskans, means tenderfoot or greenhorn (derived from the Indian words *chee,* meaning new or fresh and *chako,* which means to come or approach).

Diamond willow is a plant disease that affects branches of various species of willow, resulting in a diamond-shaped pattern that appears in the wood.

Eskimo ice cream is a native delicacy, traditionally made of whipped berries, seal oil, and snow; sometimes shortening, raisins, and sugar are added or substituted. A classic food popular throughout Alaska.

The largest gold nugget ever found in Alaska was discovered near Nome. It weighed 107 ounces, 2 pennyweight. Found September 29, 1901, it was 7 inches long, 4 inches wide and 2 inches thick.

The ice worms, usually regarded as fictitious, are actually small, thin, segmented black worms, less than one inch long, that thrive at temperatures just above freezing. They come out at dawn or dusk or on cloudy days, but when the sunlight strikes them, they burrow back down into the ice.

The igloo is an Alaskan dwelling usually made of driftwood, whalebone, and sod. It is the Canadian Eskimos, not Alaskan, who built the house of snow and ice.

Other than English, Alaskan languages include Haida, Tlingit, Tsimshian, Aleut, several dialects of Eskimo, and Athabascan.

There are 25 species of mosquitoes found in Alaska. The females feed on people, mammals, and birds. No Alaskan mosquitoes carry diseases. They are present from April to September.

Squaw candy is smoked or dried salmon. It is a very chewy food staple in winter, for Alaskans and their dogs.

The pipeline is 800 miles long, about one half is buried, the rest is on supports. It is 48 inches in diameter, with a 1.16 million barrel a day capacity.

The state capital is Juneau, which also has the largest area of any Alaskan city: 3,108 square miles.

The median age of Alaskans is 22.

Men are 54 per cent of population.

Women are 46 per cent of population.

Natives are 17 per cent of the population.

Alaska is the largest state in the Union, one fifth the size of the contiguous United States, with 586,412 square miles (or 345 million acres).

Alaska has the smallest population of any state in the United States. The largest city is Anchorage, with 197,000 people.

Alaska has four time zones and six climate zones.

Alaska has the easternmost point and westernmost point in the United States.

Alaska has the tallest mountain in North America: Mount McKinley, at 20,320 feet.

Alaska has the northernmost city in North America: Barrow.

Alaska has the deepest snowfall in one season ever recorded in North America: 81 feet.

Alaska has the longest day in the year in the U.S.: no sunset for 82 days.

Alaska has the longest night in the year in the U.S.: no sunrise for 67 days.

Alaska has the largest reserve of fresh water in the U.S. and the longest river, the Yukon: 1,400 miles in Alaska, 1,875 total.

Alaska has the largest number of lakes in the U.S. More than two million lakes are over 20 acres in size. The largest lake, Illiamna, covers 1,000 square miles.

Alaska has more coastline than the rest of the U.S. combined.

Alaska has the largest glacier in the world, the Malspina, which covers 3,937 square kilometers (1,500 square miles)—larger than the entire country of Switzerland.

Alaska is home to the largest land carnivore in the world: the Alaskan brown bear.

Alaska is the richest source of bottom fish in the world.

Alaska is the richest salmon fishery in the world.

Alaska is the location of the most expensive privately funded construction project in history: the Trans-Alaska Oil Pipeline.

Alaska contains 33 of 36 critical minerals in commercial quantities.

Alaska has the largest reserve of coal in the United States.

Alaska has over 25 per cent of oil reserves in the United States.

Alaska is the location of the world's longest sled dog race: Iditarod, 1,049 miles.

Alaska has the largest national monument in the United States: Glacier Bay.

Alaska is the location of the two largest national forests in the United States: Tongass, 16 million acres; and Chugach, 4.8 million acres.

Alaska is the home of the heartiest, most spirited, and most resourceful individuals anywhere.

# SOLO ON THE
# YUKON AGAIN

### with more Alaskan adventures

by Helen Broomell

# TABLE OF CONTENTS II

# PREFACE

*"The only way to get to know this country (or any country), the only way, is with your body. On foot. Better yet, on hands and knees.*

Edward Abbey and Phillip Hyde, Slickrock

AND I COULD ADD: "OR BY CANOE." RETURNING FROM A SECOND TRIP DOWN Alaska's Yukon River and four months of adventuring around the great state, I find myself even more awed by what I have seen and much less awed by what I have done. Traveling alone for seven hundred miles by canoe through remote areas of wilderness brought me feelings of great exhilaration and great comfort, and I'm sure that the beauty of the country has become a part of me.

Add to that the friends that I've made from one end of the state to the other, and the result was a remarkable experience. Alaskans are the friendliest, most helpful, and most energetic people I know, and there is room in "The Great Land" for everyone to go their individual ways in mutual respect.

My thanks to all who inspired me, housed me, fed me, or helped me on my way in one way or another. And to everyone at home who followed my travels in print, another thanks. It was a fine summer.

H. B.

# MAP—ROUTES OF TRAVEL

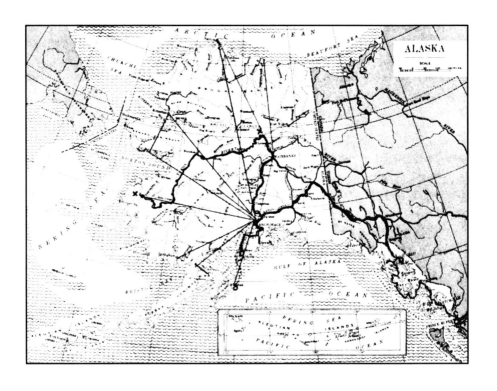

X X - canoe = light lines = plane; heavy lines = hitchhiking; O O = Alaska ferry.
750 miles      5700 miles              1300 miles                    900 miles

CHAPTER 1

# The Inside Passage

WHAT A FINE, FREE FEELING TO BE OFF AND AWAY AGAIN ON ANOTHER VISIT TO our spectacular 50th state, Alaska!

It was quite soon after returning from my last trip that I realized how strong my desire was to go back, and after corresponding for over a year with new Alaskan friends, it's good to be on my way to see new places and visit old friends.

It has been over two weeks since I left Minocqua, driving west with my brother-in-law, Bill Cameron, Sr., toward the Alaska ferry leaving from Prince Rupert, British Columbia (B.C.). Bill had corresponded with an antique car collector south of Edmonton, so that was our first destination after finding that many of the historic museums, such as Lower Fort Garry, north of Winnipeg, were not yet open.

Driving across Canada took us from winter into spring, camping all the way. It was cool and there was still ice on Tomahawk Lake when we left on May 1. Ontario was cold—no special stops through Manitoba, which was colder around Winnipeg. Then across Saskatchewan, where there was ice on the water bucket in the morning, but a few buds coming out and the trees showing green. Then Alberta, with its horizon of wheat fields and Ukrainian onion-domed churches, which brought the real change in climate and spring flowers in full bloom.

The spectacular beauty of the snowcapped mountains of B.C. will necessitate a more adequate description, as all of you who have experienced the high country well know.

A particularly interesting stop was near Hazelton, B.C., where there is a reconstructed Tlingit Indian village named 'Ksan. Although the museum wasn't open, we did visit with a young student who had learned his carving and tool-making skills at the local junior college, and was leaving that day to go to another village to teach. He was doing traditional work in large totems, as well as small boxes, dishes, and masks of museum quality. A fine thing to hear was that he had been pursuing his education for only two years, and had previously had an alcohol problem.

Trees. Hemlock I couldn't put both arms halfway around. Western red cedar and yellow cedar—huge ones. Sitka spruce so tall and straight that one can scarcely see the tops, and other varieties of spruce too.

Earlier in the trip we had the breathtaking pleasure of seeing three

*Frank Barton, a fine British Columbian*
*woodcarver, photographed at 'Ksan, B.C.*

wolves. Two ran across the road in front of our car in Riding Mountain National Park in Manitoba, and one was in the woods near our campground in Jasper National Park. We also saw a black bear, many eagles and a variety of waterfowl as we crossed the great flyways in the prairie provinces.

The weather has been hard to believe. A little rain on the drive out, but after saying goodbye to Bill in Prince Rupert on May 7, the sun shown every day for 10 days. On the western side of the Rockies, from Oregon north through Southeast Alaska, the standard weather pattern is one day of sun to four or five days of rain, mist, and fog, or any combination of those three. There was a part of one day driving in the mountains with the clouds below us for quite a while—a beautiful, ghostly sight.

Prince Rupert is a good-sized city just north of the mouth of the Skeena River and at the western end of the Yellowhead Highway, so named because a blonde Indian of mixed blood had led early explorers through the pass near Jasper, B.C., which is the route of the highway. Prince Rupert claims to be the halibut capital of the world, although the world's record, weighing 495 pounds, was caught near Petersburg. The halibut is the largest of all flatfish, and it looks very odd with both eyes on the right side of the fish.

Three days in the city gave me plenty of time to explore—it is an interesting combination of old and new, both on the waterfront and around town. Good small museum, but no small parks or benches. An old-fashioned carnival took over the city park and the great variety of nationalities made it fine for people watching.

And there are always the old-timers to talk to, with stories of the early days, although it's sometimes hard to get away from them. One 85-year-old shipbuilder and fisherman told me he had a sure cure for arthritis, and if I'd just sell him a little piece of land in Wisconsin, he would come out and cure us of arthritis. He seemed rather too fragile to make the trip. I thought he rode a bicycle, but discovered that he tied his groceries onto it in a burlap bag and pushed it the mile to his tiny shack.

The scheduled ferry to Prince Rupert had run aground somewhere north of Seattle and needed repairs, so there was a pile-up of passengers trying to get on with their vehicles. No problem for a walk-on, however, and on the morning of May 10, after having said goodbye to Bill a few days earlier, I hitched a ride to the terminal and was off on the first leg of the Southeast ferry trip up the inland passage, on another sunny day.

The Alaska Marine Highway system operates two separate routes, Southeast and Southwest, with no service connecting the two due to the heavy seas often encountered in the Gulf of Alaska. The Southeast system serves the entire panhandle from Skagway on the north to Prince Rupert, B.C., or Seattle, Washington, on the south. There are seven vessels in this fleet, the largest being the *Columbia,* which is 418 feet and carries up to 1,000 passengers. The smallest is the *Chilkat,* at 99 feet and 75 passengers. The Southwest system has two ships, the *Bartlett* and the *Tustumena,* which serve the Kenai peninsula, Kodiak Island, and occasional trips part way out the Aleutian Chain.

From the ferry we saw large areas of clear-cut forest, resembling the bare patches on the hides of moose or deer in early spring. Much of the timber is cut into cants (squared off) and shipped to Japan— some to be returned to us in other forms. There are also local pulp and sawmills. But fishing is the largest industry here, and in recent years there has been considerable replenishing of fish stock—even the big timber producers have done a lot. Fish are being tagged, and hopefully reported in when caught.

As the ferry moved toward Ketchikan, the most southerly port in Alaska, more seiners and trollers were seen, along with gillnetters. As this is tidal water, the boathouses and processing plants are built on stilts to accommodate the high tides, as are many of the houses.

Ketchikan's history goes back to the explorer Juan de Fuca, who claimed the land for Spain, but it is the ancestral home of the Tongass tribe of the Tlingit Nation. The lower Southeast is the home of the Tlingits, the Haidas, and the Tsimshians, and Ketchikan's name comes from the words *Kitsk Xaan* (the Tlingit name for the creek running through the town). The city has the largest collection of totem poles in Alaska. The Totem Heritage Center is preserving 33 original and unrestored poles, most of them between 80 and 140 years old. The stories on the totems are tied to the clan's history, their activities, where they lived, their adventures, and real or imaginary figures—not their religious beliefs, as some believe.

It was good to be off the ferry for five hours to stroll the waterfront, poke around the streets, visit with the people, and see the totem poles. It's a friendly place. They are proud of their town, and it was good to hear about the community college, where courses are taught in totem making and other crafts, as well as the usual academic courses. A unique course offered is one in marine education, which includes various aspects of commercial fishing. Their classroom, in part, is a new 44-foot fishing vessel that went into service last fall.

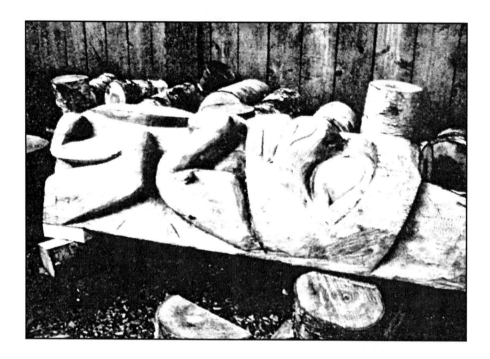

*Totem in the process.*

The following day found me in Petersburg, where everyone was preparing to celebrate Little Norway Days in honor of Norway's Independence Day on May 17. It has become quite an event over its 25 years, and this year's festival was attended by Governor Shiffield, an admiral, three mayors, a superior court judge, and many other dignitaries from around the state. Festivities included an air show, free rides on a Coast Guard cutter, a style show of new and old Norwegian dresses and clothing, dancing by the grade school students, and all kinds of events that focused on traditional Norwegian foods. What a lot to eat! One of the canneries put on a seafood buffet, with samples of all types of local seafood. The town sponsored a salmon bake on the beach, and the fraternal Sons of Norway sponsored a beautiful luncheon and style show. One family had four generations of women attired in the traditional dress, called *bunad,* worn on festive occasions only. Each geographic area of Norway has its own unique costume design.

With a week in Petersburg it was possible to settle in at the local "Tent City," a campground built on the muskeg about two miles from town, primarily for the seasonal cannery workers. Boardwalks and wooden tent platforms make it habitable, and there is a roofed shelter with washrooms and fireplaces.

The views from anywhere in Petersburg are spectacular, as snow-covered mountains form a backdrop in two directions. Just after I arrived, there was quite a commotion in town when a local fisherman came in with a 273-pound halibut which was caught (but not landed!)

*Petersburg Harbor.*

on a 25-pound test line. It was gaffed by a nearby boat and hauled to shore.

Sometime during the celebration I noticed a young girl (along with dozens of others), selling goodies along the main street; her last name was Sprague, which was my maiden name. I talked with her mother and found that her husband's family had come from Maine and that there were a number of John Spragues in his family—both similar to my own background. She invited me to dinner to meet her husband, who is a local dentist. They live across the narrows on Kupreanow Island, and have a fine, partially subsistence-type life. For dinner we had both elk steaks and fresh steelhead. They are in the process of developing a water and electric power source from a small stream coming down from the mountain across the bay from them. A fun family, with children, and one grandchild there.

Another day I spent aboard two fishing boats moored at the wharf. The project was to transfer a few tons of a Japanese delicacy consisting of kelp with herring roe attached in a heavy layer on each side—when properly cleaned it sells in Japan for the equivalent of more than $200 per pound. This catch was not top quality, but after all expenses, including rental on a 70-foot vessel, the estimated net profit was $100,000. The allowed open season is only a matter of a few hours, so it's a frantic operation, done by skilled scuba divers. The Japanese name for this delicacy is something I can neither say nor spell. It was a fascinating experience, particularly as there were only two men involved in the project, and between breaking lines in block and tackle, having to move each boat several times, and a lot of minor problems, it was quite a challenge. I operated the levers, moved pails of the stuff around, took pictures, and tried to stay out of the way. Interesting to me just to be aboard a big fishing boat.

Although not as plush as the cruise ships, these ferries are very comfortable, the food is good, and the crews are helpful. National Park Service personnel are aboard during the summer months to give talks and provide information about the area. And of course, without a car this is a very reasonable form of transportation. Senior citizens may travel free from October 1 to May 15 within the state of Alaska, although it's not necessary to be a resident to qualify. My departure date was May 10, so I rode free until the 15th. Choosing not to pay for a stateroom, I slept on the top deck, or solarium, which is sheltered but open. It's also the friendliest place to be.

The physical features of Southeast Alaska make it one of the most scenic areas of the world, quite similar to the fjords of Norway, with a chain of islands stretching from Seattle north to Glacier Bay. This similarity accounts for the settlement of Petersburg and other fishing communities in the last century by Scandinavian fishermen. The snow-covered mountains of the coastal range form a majestic backdrop for the villages along this protected waterway.

*Small fishing boat on the Inside Passage.*

The tree line in Southeast Alaska usually extends from sea level to about 3,000 feet in the southern part, and to about 1,800 feet farther north in the Icy Strait area. More then 95 per cent of the land is under federal jurisdiction. The Tongass National Forest accounts for about 75 per cent of its total area, and has been designated for multiple use. As a result, there is considerable logging and some mining being done.

A pleasant dinner and evening at the new Petersburg Senior Citizen Center completed my stay, and like all good things that have to end, the beautiful sunshine disappeared and the rains began.

Leaving Petersburg, I boarded the small ferry *Le Conte,* which took me off in the fog, westerly through Frederick Sound toward Baranof Island. Aboard ship there were a few early tourists, but the passengers were primarily local people going from one place to another. A track team traveling from their village of Kake to Juneau for a meet; brothers from Minnesota but working in Juneau, who had just paddled across Admiralty Island—mostly in the rain. A four mile portage made me lose interest in that as a possible future trip. There were people going to the doctor, visiting relatives, going to meetings, and in general just shopping and carrying on the business of living. Most were Native Tlingit Indians.

The ship docked at Sitka for an hour or so, but it was in the middle of the night, so the narrow and picturesque route through Peril Strait between Baranof and Chichagof Islands wasn't visible. The following morning, after a stop in Angoon, which is the only Native subsistence village of the Tlingit, the ferry followed Chatham Straight into Icy Strait, where I got off at the village of Hoonah. By this time the rain was coming down in a more positive way, so I put on my rain jacket, hoisted up my pack, and started the trek toward the village. Ferry terminals are usually located anywhere from one to sixteen miles (as in the case of Juneau's Auke Bay dock) out of town.

No sooner had I gotten half a mile down the road when a pickup stopped to pick me up. It was a welcome lift, much appreciated, and the offer of an empty upstairs room in the village was too good to turn down. This woman was truly a one-man chamber of commerce, and the accompanying picture shows her family. Her name is Geraldine Dick, her husband is Raymond, whom I didn't have the pleasure of meeting because he was on a return trip from the state of Washington with a fishing boat. They have three children, Margie 5, Max 8, and Regina 11. It was a real treat for me to be "adopted" into a Tlingit family for three days.

Hoonah's small white population is primarily made up of school

*Gerry Dick (with glasses) and family.*

teachers, with some mixed marriages accounting for a few more, but it is a Native Tlingit village, with a small museum, a cultural center, and a very proud heritage. They are the largest of the three Southeast tribes, the others being the Haida and the Tsimshian, and theirs is a matrilineal culture (the clan, such as raven, bear, frog, etc., is passed down on the mother's side of the family). The elders speak the native language, and it is being taught in schools.

*Houses in Hoonah at low tide.*

Hoonah has a population of about 700, which has been fairly stable since the late 1800s. The mainstay of its economy is fishing (halibut, salmon, and black cod), with only cold storage facilities in the village since the only processing plant recently closed. As a consequence, unemployment is high, and subsistence is an important part of the residents' lifestyle and cultural heritage. Most villagers rely on fish (fresh and smoked), shellfish, deer, sea mammals, and ducks and geese in season. In summer and fall people gather blueberries, salmonberries, other berries, and plants.

Considerable logging is going on in the area, both by a locally owned company and by Alaska Lumber and Pulp. Huge piles of logs and oversized trucks greeted me in my wanderings around the outskirts of town, and it was interesting to talk with the drivers. With only five miles of roads, not counting the logging trails, it didn't take me long to do it. On the steep hillsides, logging is now being done by helicopters. The Forest Service inspects all logging camps within their jurisdiction to check on cleanup and exact length of logs.

It soon became apparent to me that Gerry was more than a "meeter of ferries." She was a counselor, advisor, a friend to everyone, and an important conveyor of the Tlingit tradition. (If you're having trouble, as I did, pronouncing that tribal name, try saying *Clink-it.* That's close enough.) Our first social event was the Head Start

*Cemetery at Hoonah.*

"graduation" exercise, which reminded me of Ruby Fisher [a friend who worked with the Head Start program on the Lac du Flambeau Indian Reservation near Minocqua]; she would have enjoyed seeing the children and their fine facility there. The following evening was the high school graduation, with a big family dinner at the home of a graduating senior.

These were pleasant days, and too soon departure time arrived. Gerry gave me some home-canned salmon, the name of her husband's aunt to look up in Juneau, and a warm feeling of friendship that will always remind me of Hoonah.

The ferry trip from there to Juneau took only a few hours, but the snowcapped mountains and narrow fjords continued to provide a panorama of great beauty. We spotted two humpback whales, a school of porpoises, many eagles, and some sea lions (only visible through glasses) along the way. There were houses that were towable homes, several quite large, but all in various states of disrepair.

And the rain continues, intermittently. The weather people in Juneau say "Rain, tapering off to showers." On the ferry I met Ellen Searby, who is the author of a guide book to Southeast Alaska that I read last winter. She was working for the ferry system and was an interesting person with whom to share experiences. Local note: She taught school with Myrtle Grundy some years ago on the Papago Indian Reservation in Sells, Arizona.

The dominant features of Kluane are the two major mountain chains running parallel in a southeastern direction. Here are found some of the world's largest ice fields outside the polar regions, some dating back to the last ice age. Canada's highest peak, Mount Logan at 19,520 feet, and Mount Saint Elias, second, at 18,008 feet, are found here. Of local Minocqua area interest is the fact that Jon Ilitis, who is with the Boy Scouts High Adventure Base at Boulder Junction, Wisconsin, attempted a climb on Mount Saint Elias last year, which had to be aborted because of an avalanche that came close to tragedy for two of the group of four. He returned this past May to attempt Mount Logan; I don't know if he reached the peak, but do know there have been no lives lost on the mountain. I saw his slides of Saint Elias, and they were remarkable.

Leaving Kluane Park on the 6th day of June, I had to make a decision about my next destination. There were almost two weeks free before I needed to be in Fairbanks to meet friends. I knew that Ed Berg, who drove me to Dawson City the summer before last, and is now a permanent resident of Homer, was planning to meet his daughter and her friend in Anchorage sometime early in June, so thought it might be good timing to visit them. Hitching a ride from the Park took a few hours of waiting, which is unusual but not unexpected.

But what an unexpected treat occurred in that time! I had seen a few news blurbs about a young man who was walking from Tierra del Fuego—the tip of South America—to the Arctic Ocean, taking many years to accomplish it, but I had no idea where he was. Imagine my surprise when the park ranger looked down the road toward an orange-vested man pulling a small two-wheel cart with a pack on it, and said, "Here comes the hiker from South America!" We ran out to greet him, and being lunch time he joined us on the steps of the trailer-type park office to share a meal.

His name is George Meegan, from Kent, England, and yes, he is writing a book titled *Journey Home: A Love Story,* to be published by Putnam Sons for Christmas, 1984. Obviously, after talking with him, one realizes that, undimmed by some threatening situations in South America, he is in love with the whole human race. Really a gentle soul, with a sparkle in his eye and an almost shy demeanor. Certainly not a celebrity seeker, although in his more than five years on the road he has had his share of it. He prefers the smaller towns, and was elected honorary deputy sheriff of Iron County, Wisconsin, when he went through our part of the country. I forgot to ask him when that was. His wife accompanied him by car for the first few months of the trip, and has again joined him, staying in hotels or camping, for the last few months. His final goal is Prudhoe Bay, which is the furthest north road on the continent. After a lot of good talk and food, we said goodbye, and now I have one more reason to plan a trip to England for sometime in the future.

I had a sign for hitching to Anchorage, which was 700 miles away, and really didn't want to be off where the Tok cutoff leaves the Alaska

Highway, as I've seen dozens of hitchhikers stranded there. So, much to my great glee, a young fellow pulled up in a Datsun pickup, opened the door and called, "Anchorage Express." He was returning from a log cabin building course in the Pacific Northwest, and was off to see his sister, who lives on Kodiak Island. He will be attending the University of Minnesota at Duluth this winter, so I may see more of him.

We made it into Anchorage just ten minutes before the Youth Hostel closed for the night at 11 o'clock. A hot shower and a bed were much-appreciated luxuries. Although I would choose to avoid the city, it seems to be a necessary connecting point for many places in Alaska. There are only three roads out of Anchorage, one being the way I came in from the Alaska Highway by way of Glenalleu; one directly north to Denali Park (Mount McKinley), Fairbanks, and the pipeline road, which is closed to the public in the northern portion; and the route south to the Kenai Peninsula, which divides and goes to Seward and Homer. In the two years since I visited Anchorage last, there has been much new building and a general influx of people, so with no extra time at this point, I postponed calling people with whom I want to get in touch.

My usual good fortune held when I phoned Ed Berg, was referred to an Anchorage number, and discovered that he had picked up his daughter Tanya and her friend Kira at the airport (they live in Madison, Wisconsin), and was leaving for Homer later that day. So back into the big brown van with memories of the trip north from Minocqua two years ago still fresh in my mind. With 180,000 miles on the van and five or six trips on the Alaska Highway to its credit, it has done well to hold together.

The 200-mile trip to Homer was split into two days, as Ed was enrolled in a botany class at the Seldovia area junior college. The class meets once a week for a full day, so while the girls amused themselves, I joined the class and picked up a lot of good information about identifying Alaskan plants. The spring flowers were all in bloom and the exploratory walks with the class along the Kenai River and through the woods added to the enjoyment of the class.This is a new school located several miles out of town, and no one but me paid any attention to the fact that the moose tracks came right up to the doors of the building! Imagine pushing open a big glass door into the face of a moose?

We camped that night on the Kenai River, which by morning was filled with fishermen, and after the class drove on to Homer. Many moose along the road, including a cow with two very young calves.

The natural beauty of the Homer area is almost mind boggling. With the snowcapped Kenai Mountains and the glaciers rising up from the opposite shore of Kachemak Bay, it's no wonder that Homer, with its famous six-mile-long spit extending into the Bay, is a prime location for tourists, fishermen, and new settlers. Ed moved here just over a year ago, bought a small house, and has done considerable remodeling and fixing up, and now has a five-room home, some of which could be made into a separate apartment.

Impressions of Homer: Busy small town, but no one really in a hurry. Old cars and trucks spreading dust everywhere as new roads are being constructed and old ones repaired. Russians (Old Believers), in town by boat or car from their villages, attired in their colorful peasant-type dresses and blouses. Small groups of young people visiting in the sunshine. Many dogs. Many people leaving town for cannery jobs in Kodiak or Seward—many just arriving to set up housekeeping in a tent on the Spit, and incidentally to look for work here. And as in most of Alaska, everything seems to be in the process of being built, being fixed, or falling apart.

A long-awaited experience came to life when Ed suggested that we charter a boat to take us across the bay to Kachemak State Park to do some backpacking there for a few days. There is a small community at Halibut Cove, made up of a few families, fishermen, resort operators, and an outfitter who uses llamas quite successfully for short trips or expeditions in the mountains. The park covers over 300,000 acres of wilderness and is only accessible by boat or plane. It is an undeveloped area, although there is a volunteer ranger at Halibut Cove who, interestingly, is a retired sea captain from Prince Edward Island on Canada's east coast, who walked across Canada to the Pacific before coming to Alaska. Interesting people in this great country. The ride across the bay takes about 45 minutes with a high-powered outboard and a heavy skiff. Wouldn't want to try it in a rowboat.

Good weather stayed with us throughout the trip, although the last day was overcast, with droplets of mist falling on us so gently that we didn't feel them—could only see them on the quiet water. The hike up toward Leisure Lake was steep at times, but there was a trail, and except for an occasional bout with the huge spiney-thorny Devil's Club, we had no trouble reaching a fine campsite on the lake in time for dinner. I found shelter under the thick boughs of a large, friendly spruce tree, as I also had done in Kluane Park, and rolled out my pad and sleeping bag in its bivvy sack for a perfectly dry night's sleep in spite of a light rain around me.

The location beside a stream coming into the lake was so perfect that we decided to use it as a base camp for the following few days. An added reason was that the ranger had mentioned a canoe that had been stashed in the alders nearby, and that we should feel free to use it. Which we did. By portaging into the next lake we could paddle into two more small lakes. The loons greeted us in each lake. I've never known water so clear or so cold, and with the white-capped peaks reflected in it, each lake was a perfect gem.

The girls and Ed climbed Poot Peak, the smallest and most accessible of the mountains, but it was a tough one, with some of the climbing in snow fields, and, above tree line, rock climbing. When we returned to the Bay to be picked up after four days, the salmon were running, the water was full of boats, and the shore was lined with fishermen snagging for the big kings. True sportsmen frown on this method of catching them by casting with large treble hooks.

The boat trip back to Homer was a rough and windy one, highlighted for me by a flock of murres that flew over us. They rather resemble small penguins, but with a longer neck and tail. We arrived at the house to find the cat had had three kittens in our absence, and the three-month-old lab pup had perfected her chewing skills considerably. Both in the care of Ed's nephew, Jim, who lives with him.

Juneau is a city built on gold. Originally the site of a Tlingit fishing camp, it became a rowdy placer mining camp in 1880 when gold was discovered there by Joe Juneau and Richard Harris. The site later became the world's largest low-grade gold mining operation in the world, and later, the capital of Alaska. With a present population of about 22,000, Juneau is the third-largest city in Alaska, and with voters in the state rejecting the estimated 2.84 billion dollar cost of moving the capital to a location north of Anchorage, the future of the city seems assured. There is no road access to Juneau, and for this reason the capital move has been on the ballot a number of times. According to one government study, 85 per cent of Juneau's total economy and population revolves around the presence of the state capital. Government is big business.

The mountain wilderness is at the city's back door, quite literally, and the Mendenhall Glacier, a 3,000-year-old river of ice, flows a few feet a day into the Mendenhall River a few miles out of town. Along this river, the city has spread its rapidly growing population, so that the valley has become a crowded suburb with many problems.

My four days in Juneau were exciting and interesting, thanks to people who recommended friends with whom I could visit. Mary Shields (friend from my 1981 trip) gave me the name of Deborah Vogt, who lives across the bridge over the Gastineau Channel, in the town of Douglas. Deb had formerly lived in a log cabin outside of Fairbanks before deciding to return to law school. She is now an assistant attorney general for the state of Alaska. Quite different from her life "in the bush."

Days were spent sightseeing and evenings socializing. There is much to do of both in Juneau, and I was glad to have more time there than I did two years ago. The museum is the finest in the state, and was showing a traveling exhibit from the Smithsonian of old Bering Sea Eskimo art and artifacts. The Governor's Mansion, the old Russian Orthodox Church, and a trip out to the remains of the old gold mine were highlights, along with the glacier, but I seem to enjoy most just walking around, soaking up the atmosphere, and talking to the people.

It's possible, in Juneau, to walk about three blocks almost straight up the mountainside by way of a series of steps. The views are excellent. Through Helen Wright, of Rhinelander, Wisconsin, I had the pleasure of meeting Judy Cooper, a local artist, musician, highway construction worker, and general advisor to young city recreation workers. Her house, part way up the hillside, reflected both her artistic skills and her warmth. I also had lunch with a young couple, Dave and Peggy Pijan, whose parents live in Wausau, Wisconsin, who were house-sitting for a woman in Juneau. Their home is a cabin in the bush where they've lived a number of years— only accessible by plane. Not enough time with them.

Another pleasant memory of Juneau was dinner with Gerry Dick's relatives, who live in the town of Auke Bay, near the ferry terminal. Their home is a large, new log cabin, which was easy to spot from the city bus. After supper and a lot of good conversation, we suddenly realized that it was almost departure time for the ferry. So began the last leg of my adventures by boat.

The long summer days of Alaska are moving up on us, even this far south in the state, so when the ferry left Juneau at 8 p.m., there were still several hours of daylight left. Arrival time in Skagway was 2 a.m., so I was glad that, for once, the ferry dock was only a few blocks from town and a place called the Bunkhouse, where for a few dollars one could roll out a sleeping bag and have hot showers.

Skagway, Alaska, is unique. It's a step back in time, with reminders of the Gold Rush days of 1898 visible everywhere. Most of the early buildings are intact, have been refurbished, and house the stores and restaurants that serve the town. In recent years, the National Park Service has taken over the restoration of a number of historic buildings in Skagway, as well as the supervision and maintenance of the Chilkoot Trail, which is the 33-mile "Trail of '98," which led the gold seekers over the pass to Lake Bennett, where they traveled the Yukon River to Dawson and the Klondike gold fields. The trail is littered with reminders of the tortuous route, where every stampeder had to carry one ton of equipment and goods (a year's supply) in order to be admitted into Canada at the border.

The population of Skagway in 1898 approached 12,000, with hotels, saloons, shops, gambling halls, and brothels lining the streets. It was a wild and lawless town. The White Pass and Yukon Railroad was completed at that time and ran continuously, serving the mines, hauling freight, and carrying passengers (and cars and trucks) until October, 1982, when the mines closed and tourist revenue was insufficient to continue operation. It was probably one of the most famous narrow gauge railroads in the world. Its closing down has been a blow to the local economy, but the cruise ships still come in, and with a new road to Whitehorse and more excursion boats, it may be possible to make up for the loss of the train. There are hopes for its return in 1984.

My arrival in Skagway was well timed, as there was a small cruise ship in port for a demonstration to the local chamber of commerce and business people of what they were offering the tourists this summer. I was invited and joined the group for a cocktail cruise to the town of Haines, entertainment on board, and lots of interesting people to meet during the two-hour trip. Following that, the local theatrical group put on their first showing (complimentary to the townspeople) of *The Days of '98,* a fine historical presentation of the story of Soapy Smith and the lawlessness of the gold rush days.

Eventually the sun came out and I moved from the Bunkhouse to the town campground in order to save a few dollars and be outdoors. It's about half a mile out of town, so is convenient. I met a charming girl, Madeline Rizk, who had just flown in from her job as a teacher in the tiny Alaskan bush community of Toksook Bay, on the Bering Sea. It was fascinating to share experiences with her, and when her friend Beverly arrived with Gordon Castanza, there were even more great stories going around. Beverly also taught in a small Eskimo village, and Gordon, who is involved in electronics, ran the 1981 Iditarod Sled Dog Race. He plans to do it again in 1984.

I had hoped to hike out of Skagway by way of the Chilkoot Pass, following the route of the Klondike Gold Rush of '98. The National Park people had traversed the route, which is a four-day hike in good weather, and told me that unless I had snowshoes, it would be a foolhardy venture. So they didn't have to talk very hard to persuade me not to try the pass this early in the season, and I substituted several shorter hikes around the area instead.

In the ten days I spent in Skagway, the lasting impressions are the sense of history one feels, the friendliness of the people (average age must be under 30), the almost constant wind swooping down the mountain sides rattling loose boards and scattering dust, and the interesting parade of people of all nationalities who swarm off the cruise ships for an overnight stop, making people watching into a favorite local activity.

CHAPTER 2

# North to
# Southern Alaska

Among the friends I met in Skagway were the owners of the local hack service, Dan and Michele Keny. They have buggies and wagons drawn by impeccably groomed ponies that meet the ships and tour groups arriving in town, offering transportation or just sightseeing. Fortunately for me, they were driving to Whitehorse, which is the only road out of town, and offered to take me along. It was a beautiful 125-mile drive. We reached the Canadian border into Yukon Territory in a short time, then the summit at White Pass, where large areas of snow covering the rocky treeless landscape were reflected in the crystal-clear alpine lakes. Spring had barely arrived in this cold and barren area, but willows and tiny plants were showing buds.

*White Pass between Skagway and Whithorse,*
*along the new highway.*

At Lake Bennett, which is a headwaters of the Yukon River, we were reminded of the many hundreds of gold rush stampeders who stopped there to make the boats to carry them on down the river a thousand miles to Dawson and the gold fields. Many lost their lives in the tortuous rapids near Whitehorse.

Further on the road, near the village of Carcross (population 150), lies the so-called "world's smallest desert." It's an interesting expanse of sand dunes and sparse desert-like vegetation. The town cemetery, besides being the final resting place of the two Indians who first discovered gold on Bonanza Creek with George Carmack, is also the burial place of the famous Polly, a parrot that reportedly was brought over the Chilkoot Pass in 1898. When Polly died in the mid-'70s, she was given a full funeral, and her demise at well over a hundred years was reported in many magazines and newspapers.

Because we had gotten a fairly early start, we arrived in Whitehorse before lunch, so I had plenty of time to sightsee around town before meeting Dan and Michele late afternoon. They were going out of town to a hot springs campground to spend the night, which was on my route also, though my road branched off before the hot springs.

Although I had stopped in the city on my first trip to Alaska two years ago, there was much I didn't see. Whitehorse is the capital of Yukon Territory, and two-thirds of the entire population of the province resides there. The last of the sternwheelers, SS *Klondike,* which was built in 1929, has been restored and is a National Historic Site of Parks Canada in Whitehorse. There were altogether some 250 such sternwheelers constructed for use on the Yukon River and its tributaries between 1866 and 1936. Another, the SS *Keno,* is on display in Dawson City. These steam-powered boats were the Yukon's primary transportation system for almost four generations. The SS *Klondike*'s career as a cargo vessel came to an end in 1950, with the opening of an all-weather road between Whitehorse and the silver-lead ore mines at Mayo. The White Pass and Yukon Railroad carried cargo from 1900 on and provided ocean access from the interior. Parks Canada does a very realistic job of restoration on their historic sites. Some bunks were left unmade, the pilot house has cookies and coffee on the wood stove, the galley is complete with foods (fake of course), and boxes and cargo are labeled from the '40s. The ship had a capacity of 300 tons, including tremendous amounts of wood to fire the boilers, which had to be replenished every 24 hours or less. The

Yukon River is now quiet and of little interest commercially, except to the salmon fishermen—very different from the earlier years.

The following night I spent close to Yukon's Kluane National Park, after getting a ride with a group of fishermen to a campsite near Haines Junction. My immediate destination was to the Kluane Park area to hike, so the following morning, after checking with the Park Service and watching the award-winning slide show about the park, I got a ride to the base of Sheep Mountain on Kluane Lake and started hiking. Didn't see any Dall sheep on the mountain, as it was lambing time so the ewes weren't in sight, and the rams had gone to the other side. But the scenery was spectacular, with snow-covered peaks in almost every direction, and glaciers and ice fields in the far distance forming rivers that make impossible barriers to the foot traveler. There were bear, wolf, and moose signs everywhere; although I didn't see the animals, I felt they weren't far away.

CHAPTER 3

# Reunions
# in Fairbanks

# SOLO ON THE YUKON AGAIN

WITH A PROMISE TO RETURN TO VISIT FRIENDS IN THE HOMER AREA IN LATE August, I joined two women who were driving to Fairbanks. Their destination was the Midnight Sun Writers Conference at the University of Alaska, and mine was to visit my friends—Celia Hunter and Ginny Wood, among others, with whom I had stayed two years ago at the time of my first Yukon River trip. After that I will hitch north to retrieve my canoe, which has been watched over by the owner of the truck stop at the pipeline bridge, about a hundred miles north of Fairbanks. Then I'll travel *(float,* they say in Alaska) as far toward the Bering Sea as I want to go. That will depend on weather—wind, primarily, as rain or cold aren't hazards. I may go as far as St. Mary's, or I may go only to Holy Cross. No schedules, no plans, seems to work well for me, and I'm sure that staying open to anything that comes along is what makes my travels so interesting. How fortunate that I have the time to do it!

It was a two~day trip to Fairbanks, with warm, sunny days continuing. Salmon season had recently opened on the Kenai Peninsula, so there were hundreds of campers, trucks, and all kinds of vehicles heading for favorite fishing spots all along the way. Traveling north from Homer along the west shore of Cook Inlet, we had a clear view across the bay of the 10,000-foot volcanoes, Mount Iliamna and Mount Redoubt, though not as spectacular as the Kenai Mountains across Kachemak Bay from Homer. At Kenai, the road turns inland to go through parts of the Kenai National Wildlife Refuge, where moose are almost as common as dogs. We met a cow moose with her two small calves crossing the road not far from Moose Pass.

Accompanying us in the van were two large white dogs, one a Samoyed and the other a mix of Samoyed and Great Pyrenees, who brought back memories of my own Pyrenees dogs. Fun to ride with them in spite of the warm weather and the shedding wooly coats. Caroline Coons, who drove, is an interesting person. Approaching 80, she is a strong and vibrant personality, ready for new challenges and interests, and with a wealth of stories and history of the early days in Alaska. She was a much-loved school teacher in Nome for many years. Joy Griffin, our third member, recently retired to Homer with her husband, and also tells interesting stories of life in bush Alaska.

The new highway along Twinagain Arm, where a disappointed Captain Cook had to backtrack in his early explorations of the area, is a beautiful drive. It shares space just above the high-tide line with the railroad, goes along the base of high cliffs, beside wetland bird sanctuaries, and gives a view of Portage glacier.

Going north from Anchorage to Fairbanks, the Alaska Railroad, which runs parallel to the highway, is famous for its scenery and its history. I took the railroad trip two years ago, so was glad to travel it by car. We camped south of Denali Park, but drove in to the hotel there for midmorning coffee. The weather was spectacular again, and although many people come to see Mount McKinley only to find it under clouds, we had watched it for a part of two days as we drove north—a magnificent sight. The entire Alaska Range, because it extends over so much of the south central part of the state, brings mountains and glaciers close to much of the sparse highway system. Even from Fairbanks, we can, on a clear day, see Mount McKinley, which is more than 150 miles away.

Returning to Fairbanks was like coming home for me. Celia Hunter and Ginny Wood had been most hospitable in '81, and after corresponding over two winters since, I was glad to be back in their log cabin home outside of town. I found them both involved in typical occupations and duties for the time of year. With the gardens all planted, Ginny was erecting a second, bigger and heavier moose fence around the largest garden. Last summer a cow brought her calf into it to enjoy the luscious vegetables and strawberries. Ginny figured that, as moose are good high-jumpers, but poor broad jumpers, she would build another fence four feet behind the first, and hope that would solve the problem. Now both gardens look like "Fort Vamoose." Celia was building steps to a new storage building that is beautiful enough to live in, and completing that, we went on to repair some plumbing. They have improved and insulated the chicken house, so their twenty chickens and four turkeys can be comfortable later in the fall. They also purchase fish very reasonably from a local Native who operates a nearby fish wheel, so their store-bought food purchases are minimal. This is a way of life for many Alaskans, some because of choice and for others a matter of necessity.

The summer solstice (longest day of the year) is cause for great celebration in Alaska, and young and old gather for fairs, festivals, and parties to mark the occasion. It's odd to have it light all night, and not unusual to find people working outdoors at eleven o'clock, or to see children still playing at midnight. The sun seems to give extra energy to people as well as plants, and there are downtown sidewalk sales with stores open until midnight. The university has special events also.

Most of my free time in Fairbanks has been spent visiting people I met two years ago. A young pilot and his wife, Ken and Lindy Couch, whom I met in Fort Yukon, have since moved to North Pole, a town north of Fairbanks, and have a baby girl. Lindy invited me out to lunch with her mother and other members of her family. My first "fancy" meal out, and much appreciated. Ken and Lindy were just recovering from the loss in a violent windstorm of a small plane they had just purchased (not new). The motor had been removed for repair, so without the weight, the plane was more vulnerable. To make matters worse, it was uninsured. So they were disappointed not to be able to take us all "flight-seeing" around the area.

A few days later, Carol Kasza, who with her husband Jim Campbell led the backpacking trip I went on two years ago, stopped in for a visit with her year-old daughter and her parents. Good to see them. My friend Jan Schofield, who has kept in touch since we met in Homer two years ago, was also in Fairbanks for the writers conference, so we've spent time together. I've caught up on news of their new log cabin across the bay from Homer, and what's going on in their lives.

Jan's husband Ed has completed the cabin (well, almost completed —hardly anyone ever really finishes a place in Alaska), even to getting the cupboards in, so I'll be glad to see it when I visit them in late August. They are accessible by ferry from Homer once a week, or by plane to Seldovia. The cabin is fourteen miles out of town on a logging road. Last fall the company stopped logging and maintaining the roads, so when a bridge washed out, the Schofields were stranded. In true community style, the good people of the village came to their rescue and rebuilt the bridge so they could get out.

Earlier in the year a baby seal had washed ashore near the

Schofields, umbilical cord still attached. They nursed it long enough to save its life and kept it for a time before taking it to a friend who cares for homeless animals. He was recently featured in an article by Jan in the *Anchorage Daily News,* with a full-color picture of the baby seal. Christened Herriott, the baby was irresistible, with its big brown eyes and affection for Jan, its substitute mother.

Jan has published an Alaskan coloring book, now in its second printing. It's a fine book for children, with her own drawings and lots of excellent information about Alaska in it. She's now working on an Alaskan wild edible plant book.

Weather in Fairbanks has been very warm—in the 80s, and hovering around 90 degrees for several days, so when my other good friends, Mary Shields and John Manthei, called to suggest a few days on the river here, I was delighted. John's sister is Sue Pucci, an artist from St. Germain, Wisconsin, who suggested that I get in touch with them two years ago. Mary, originally from Racine, Wisconsin, was one of the first women to run the thousand-mile Iditarod sled dog race, and both she and John have had dog teams for many years. Mary has been heard on National Public Radio talking about life in the North, and has now completed a book on dogsledding, which is to be published by Alaska Northwest Publishing Company.

Accompanied by Mary's retired lead dog Cabbage, now a house pet, we drove just out of town to where the Chena River joins the Tanana, pulled into a driveway, and it was obviously a toss-up who was most anxious to get on the water—could well have been Cabbage. But we couldn't start before visiting with John Verbeek and his wife. John has been a dog musher for many years, often on long trips alone in the Brooks Range, and now has about twenty dogs. He tells great stories and helps sponsor Iditarod racers.

When running rivers here, it's done with a good outboard motor so the return trip upstream can be made. Not many places where there is road access. Ours was a twenty-foot aluminum canoe with a motor mount, so there was plenty of room for all of us and no concern about stability. The river was moving at a good rate. I'd estimate 8 or 10 mph, and with no desire to run the motor until we needed it, we floated as fast as we could have paddled. Past old cabins on the river,

*Typical river cabin. Note some sod still on the roof.*

past new cabins, past dog teams, past a derelict sternwheeler, and past four or five air boats, which, when running, tend to make one think of being enclosed inside a jet motor in a very small room.

The water seemed warm enough for a swim, so John and Mary jumped out and swam alongside the canoe for a few hundred yards, while Cabbage and I floated with them. After a few miles we joined the Tanana River, and were quickly away from civilization except for a few homes high on the hills and a few old cabins near the water. At one point we had a clear view of the area which had recently been part of the Rosy Creek forest fire, where it spread along the Parks Highway south of Fairbanks. The Tanana is a different kind of river, as it has the silty, milky water that has come from the glaciers far away. Not what one would choose to swim in, but similar to the Yukon. Where the Chena and the Tanana come together, it resembles cream being poured into coffee.

Lunch was a picnic on the river bank. We found a good breeze, but no shade, and enjoyed crackers and cheese, home-dried salmon jerky, salad greens from the garden, and lemonade. Cabbage enjoyed a run and the salmon skins.

John and Mary know many people along the river, and have netted salmon on the Tanana for several years. The season will open soon, so everyone is getting their nets ready, although Native fisher-men have no regulations, so their nets and fish wheels are out. The picture on page 44gives a good idea of how a fish wheel operates. The basic principle is akin to a perpetual motion machine. The baskets are kept turning by the current. Salmon swim against the current when migrating, and as a result, approach the revolving wheel over the sides of the basket. The basket comes up under the fish, carries it free of the water, and as the basket approaches its vertical point, the fish slides downward toward the axle to the angled trough, and then into the box at the base of the wheel.

Contrary to common belief, the fish wheel was not invented by Alaskan Indians or Eskimos. It originated on the east coast of the U.S. and later became popular in the Pacific Northwest. Operators who sell fish must have a commercial license, and early on the Chena River we passed the wheel that supplies the fish for Celia and Ginny.

Campsites weren't plentiful when the desires of the small group included: one, a breeze; two, shade; three, firewood; and four, natural beauty, which would have been hard not to find. We settled on almost an island in a marshy, tussock-covered area of emerald green equisetum, which had patches of cotton grass growing in it and a fringe of black spruce in the background. The island itself was beautiful, with spruce as large as any I've seen anywhere. I could barely get my arms two-thirds of the way around the one I slept under, and there were more like it, making the forest floor clear of underbrush and full of blooming bunchberries, twin flowers, leatherleaf, Labrador tea, and all kinds of lovely spring blooms. The sunlight filtered in through the branches and gave the whole island the feeling of a cathedral. Indeed it was.

A dinner of mooseburgers and trimmings finished off a lovely day, and with the sun down and the mosquitoes not too bad, it was comfortable to go to bed. The noises of the night were various. We had noted that beavers were working all along the river, often cutting down large cottonwood trees in favor of the smaller aspen, so weren't surprised to hear the familiar slap of the beaver tail on the water. Another similar sound, repeated many times during the night, was the splash of chunks of river bank eroding away and falling into the water with a loud plop!

The next day we started early, after a breakfast of fried eggs, bacon, and toast, and paddled on down the river for some miles, investigating anything of interest along the way. The destination was a small river that flows into the Tanana at a particularly beautiful spot. The approach was tricky, due to "sweepers" (trees whose roots have been dislodged and have fallen into the river at right angles)—and "preachers" (dead heads that have lodged in the current, which bob up and down, as a preacher praying). It was a joy to find a good campsite that had been well cared for by the public—I would have enjoyed more time there. However, as Mary and John had to get back, and going upstream with the motor requires both time and attention, we gave Cabbage a good run and started the return trip. No problems, although the amount of debris floating down the river is tremendous, including whole trees and large logs that have been washed off the sandbars. The water is high now because the hot weather and bright sun has melted the snow on the glaciers.

We passed the SS *Discovery,* a sternwheeler that has been restored to its original condition by the Binkley family, and has operated as a tourist attraction for many years. They are good people, and it is a pleasant trip upriver to where the passengers disembark to visit a fish wheel, log cabin, and generally poke around an oversized exhibit of bush Alaska mementos.

These few days on the Tanana made me eager to get to the Yukon River, so it was a relief to return to Fairbanks, call Ken Mendez at the truck stop where my canoe was left, and find that it was safely awaiting my arrival.

CHAPTER 4

# Return
# to the River

BACK ON THE HIGHWAY AGAIN! BUT THIS TIME FOR A SHORTER TRIP, AND ONE that was familiar because I did it in reverse in '81 when I paddled from Dawson to the pipeline bridge. Celia and Ginny dropped me off north of Fairbanks, where the highway starts. Four hundred fifteen miles later it ends at Prudhoe Bay on the Arctic coast, making it the furthest north road in this hemisphere. Apparently a Duluth pack,

*It wasn't a long wait.*

two other small packs, and a sign reading "Yukon River" didn't scare everyone off, as I was picked up within 15 minutes by a young man who had just moved up from Georgia. He was a country music trucker. The road has been improved in the past two years, and the trip of several hours went by quickly. Alaska's highway department mixes red and yellow poppyseed with the grass and whatever else they use for ground cover. The effect is startlingly beautiful. Two rigorous winters didn't damage the aluminum canoe that "Dave the Certified Welder" in Woodruff, Wisconsin had reduced from a 17-foot boat to a 15-foot one for me. Ken Mendez, who owns the truck stop at the junction of the Yukon and the highway, has enlarged and diversified his business, and was correct in saying that I wouldn't recognize it. We talked over a cup of coffee, then he hosed out the canoe and towed it down to the river with his three-wheeler.

It was good to be back on the Yukon again. Like meeting an old friend, it seemed as if no time had elapsed since our last visit, and we started in right where we left off the last time. With no having to get acquainted necessary, I was free to start enjoying the trip from the moment I got on the water. This is a busy time on the river. Salmon fishing is just about at its peak, and there are many more nets out, and more fish wheels operating, than I saw before. The season is open and closed on different days of the week on different parts of the river, which does complicate matters for the fisherman.

There are many differences between being on the Yukon and paddling Wisconsin or Ontario rivers and lakes, but some of the more interesting are worth mentioning. First, of course, is its size— over 1,500 miles long, starting in British Columbia. In the 600 miles that I covered in '81, the width didn't vary much, except as it ran through the Yukon Flats. There it braided out into meandering channels that covered a width of fifteen miles. Now the river is about one-half to one mile across, though islands and sloughs can cover a greater area, making various alternative routes possible. It's often a toss-up whether, in a wind, the longer more protected route is better than staying in the stronger current and battling the wind. Usually I opt for the former, but there are times when that isn't practical.

Another difference is the terrain, which is much more rugged,

*A mile across and a good wind.*

and the rocks here are much more sharp. An advantage for Alaska, however, is the all-night summer daylight. Combined with the current, there's no reason for not drifting on if a person has trouble finding a campsite. Good campsites are rare. Shorelines are a mix of cliffs or bluffs, cut banks that are a tangle of fallen trees and muck, large expanses of wetlands that are fine for waterfowl, and slanting rocky shores that have few level spots. The good old gravel bars from earlier on the river have become mud bars, making camping impossible. The best sites, of course, have been taken by the fish camps. Some are temporary tents, cleaning tables, and drying racks, but many are permanent log cabins with more facilities.

The weather has been a bit of everything, but mostly sunny and hot. There have been brief thundershowers that pass in half an hour, some bringing heavy winds and forcing me to run for shelter along the shore. At one time, repeated thunderstorms brought not only lightning, but hail that bounced in my aluminum canoe like cannonballs and on my head like golfballs. Didn't last long. Following that storm, more of the riverbanks fell into the water, making a lot of noise. But only once in the past two weeks has there been a long, extended rain, which proved again that I have a fine tent and good waterproof gear for me and my equipment. There's nothing as comfortable as curling up in a snug down bag and listening to the sound of the rain on the tent, knowing that all will be dry in the morning. The skies have been more beautiful than I remembered, with sometimes half the sky bright blue with fluffy white clouds, and the other half black and threatening. There is more than the usual haze over the distant mountains, as fires have been burning in this area too, and much blackened debris has come floating down the river. The pungent smell of woodsmoke was with me for days, not the unpleasant wet burned wood odor, but a much more pleasant aroma. Could be a combination of forest fires, salmon being smoked for hundreds of miles up and down the river, and the natural aromatic vegetation of the area mixed in.

The first village stop was in Rampart, where at one time there was a lot of talk about building a hydroelectric dam. Fortunately for those of us who like our rivers natural, and others whose livelihood was threatened, the project was defeated. But other rivers are being considered. Rampart, sixty miles from the bridge, is a small native village, with a multimillion-dollar school under construction there, although there is only one small cabin store and post office combination. It was a hot day when I was there, and it seemed as if all the children in town were squeezing into a large skiff to go a short way down the river for a swim. There are eddy pools all along the river, and this was a large one with full-length driftwood trees conveniently in place on the beach, under some fine big willow trees.

On down the river a few miles, I was met by a young man who invited me to come to visit his mother and a friend at their cabin. I was having a hard time finding a campsite, so gladly accepted the invitation. They live in Fairbanks, but have a permanent fish camp on the river. Their name is Kokrine, and Bobby's grandfather was an early Russian settler in the area for which the Kokrine Hills and the town of Kokrine were named. (The town is now abandoned, though I visited the cemetery.) His mother, Effie, is a Native woman who has spent all her life in the area. A friend of her daughter's was visiting in order to help out during fishing season. For supper I had my first meal of fish heads. It's a custom among these Indians to eat the heads first, and with salmon there's quite a lot of meat, but I'll have to confess to passing on the eyes! It was comfortable sleeping on their sofa and I enjoyed visiting with them.

Imagine my surprise when I was greeted the following day on the river by an Alaska State patrolman! In the first place, I didn't know they were on the river at all, and in the second place, he was in an unmarked boat. I was somewhat fearful when he said, "I heard you were on the river," as I could, in a split second, think of all kinds of emergencies that might bring out the police. But then he continued to say that he just thought he'd say hello, and I was relieved. His territory is from the village of Ruby to the bridge on the river, and from the Brooks Range on the north to Denali Park on the south— and he is the only one! He was at the moment on his way to Rampart, where someone had broken into the store.

My second village stop was in Tanana (accent on the last *na,* doesn't rhyme with banana). I found a camping spot just before town, had supper, and not knowing the time because I don't have a watch, wandered toward town to see what I could find. Tanana's small population is spread out along the shore for several miles, so I was glad when a fellow named Mike, in an ancient Jeep, stopped and offered a ride. I had the name of a young man to look up for Mary Shields, and he happened to work for Mike, who then drove me around while he did some errands. Never did find Mary's friend, but enjoyed Mike and met his wife and baby and visiting in-laws instead. Mike is an RN, but lost his job when they closed the hospital there. He now spends full time running the airport, doing charters, rebuilding old planes, and in his spare time runs a dog team. He and his wife spend two months in the winter in New York City, where he is from, to "stay in touch with reality," he says. I tried to sneak out of town early the next morning, but although I had already passed Mike's place and his several dozen dogs, there were two or three teams tied by the riverbank on the other end of town. They all set up a howl you wouldn't believe, shattering the early morning quiet!

For a hundred miles or so beyond Tanana there was little activity and no villages. An occasional cluster of two or three cabins, but no evidence of life. Being a holiday weekend, the fishing was closed and everyone was in town celebrating. The firefighters, drafted from the local unemployed (which essentially means everyone), were all back in the villages too, as the fires seemed to be under control. These were excellent days for observing wildlife, with or without field glasses. A young black bear was ambling down the beach at the same speed as my canoe was drifting. I watched him playing in and out of the water for about a mile. Ravens are plentiful, and I've never before had an opportunity to watch and listen to them for any length of time. I began to understand why the raven played such an important part in the folk stories and the lives of the early Northwest Coast and Southeast Alaskan Indians. Their voices, besides the crowing sound, seem to have an almost infinite variety of sounds, sometimes as clear and bell-like as a marimba note, and at other times only a mix of gurgling, gargling, and glurping. They seem always to be arguing with the seagulls over a dead fish, or protecting their territory, or possibly (I like to think), just talking with me. One tends, when alone in the wilderness, to speak to any creature who comes along.

Early in the trip, I had the great pleasure of seeing a number of peregrine falcons just above me on the high bluff. That was near the rapids. Oh yes, there is one set of rapids on the Yukon, contrary to my earlier idea, but they were only a "rock garden" with the water flow as it is. In the spring runoff it would be a different matter. It is truly remarkable to think of a river running all across this huge state with only one bridge and one rapids. But back to the falcons: several years ago they were on the endangered species list, but I don't know their current status. There was another nesting site a few miles downstream, and I must have seen a total of fifteen birds, all very angry and noisy over my interest in them.

Bank swallows by the hundreds do their best to keep down the mosquito population. Hawks of some brown and white species perch on the very top of the black spruce and screech their objections to my presence, but when pursued by the tiny swallows they turn tail and fly. A golden eagle surveyed all he could see from an even taller spruce tree, unaware that with my field glasses, I was looking him right in the eye—an impressive sight. And I wonder what there is about a gull that makes it want to line up with others on a log, as if measured and spaced, all facing in the same direction, to go marching down the river undisturbed by anything.

So far I've seen only one moose, but that was a fun one. While paddling about a quarter of a mile out from shore early one morning, I noticed what I thought was a heavy piece of driftwood going down the river. It shouldn't have been moving so much, so with the glasses my suspicions were confirmed. The moose's ears were rotating like a radar antenna, trying to figure out what and where I was. We raced to shore, but I couldn't get closer than about thirty feet, and by the time he got out of the water, he was probably fifty feet away. There are moose and bear tracks on every shore.

*My tent was inspected by a moose.*

One of the largest fish camps on the river is operated by the Honea family of Ruby. When I came by, Valerie and her husband Arvin were being helped by another fellow and a girl, Mari Hoe, from Norway. Valerie's parents were in Ruby, where they had gone for a funeral. Mari attends the University of Alaska in Fairbanks because she is interested in sled dog racing, which is how she met Valerie, who has placed in many statewide races in the past few years. She had a beautiful team of dogs at the fish camp, and contrary to most teams, they didn't make a sound when I came in. They're accustomed to women. Mari is interested in getting people started on skiing with dogs, which is popular in Norway, and was at one time in this country.

I couldn't turn down an invitation to a lunch of moose roast, mashed potatoes, and salad, with such charming companions, so after helping them remove salmon strips from brine and hanging them to dry, we enjoyed our dinner. They had eaten breakfast at 6 a.m., and would probably have supper after work at 8 or 9 p.m. It's a long day and hard work for the length of the season. All of their catch is smoked after drying, and when I was there Arvin was making an addition to the two-story high tin-sided smokehouse.

The fish cleaning and stripping area is a new, blue, tarp-covered raft about 20 feet by 30 feet, with tables, rack, and everything they need anchored firmly to the shore. They have a small generator for power tools and a washing machine, but fresh water comes from a nearby stream by plastic hose and is gravity fed to a faucet near the house and on down the hill to the fish house. The log cabin there belongs to Valerie's parents, but there is a smaller one next door that was built by the four fellows who floated the Yukon on a raft several years ago for the National Geographic Society. There was an article in the magazine and a TV special on the trip. No Alaskan native would paint the front door to his bush cabin fire-engine red. But it did look pretty in the pictures. It's a good cabin, and the girls live there now. I stopped to see the Honea winter camp about four miles down the river in a more protected, woodsy area. Their fish wheel is located there, and it must be the largest one on the river. It's the only one I've seen with three baskets instead of the customary two, and being larger, can reach deeper into the river for the larger salmon. They've

*Large, three-basket fish wheel, owned by the Honeas of Ruby.*

taken as much as 350 pounds from the wheel at a time.

In the village of Ruby, I looked up Mary Shield's friends, Dolly and Albert Yrjana (pronounced Iriana), with whom she had stayed some years ago during the Iditarod race, and Altona Brown, the eldest of the Native women in town. She has had a third pacemaker, and is going strong at something over 80 years of age. Albert immigrated to Alaska before the Matanuska Valley settlement deal of the '30s. He came from a farm near Houghton, Michigan, and except for one trip back there soon after, just to be sure it had been the right decision, he hasn't left Alaska for fifty years. His wife, Dolly, was a Canadian, and has been a lifelong friend of Altona's.

When Altona noticed that it looked like rain, she suggested that I stay over and sleep on her sofa, which was just fine with me, as I was eager to hear more of her life. She lives in a new house, which was built for her by her family, next door to her old one. And of course, she complains because it's too small, but it's nice, and she is a good housekeeper. A rare thing to see in the villages. Not only that, but she gardens, runs her own skiff, could easily shoot a moose or a bear, is tanning two hides now, makes mukluks, does beadwork, and to top it all off, she looks and acts only 60. She also speaks her own mind, and obviously is a very strong woman. We sat up late (for me) talking, and she told me much of the history of her life. When she was quite young, she contracted polio during one of the epidemics early in the century. She remembers well the pain and the care given by her parents and her older brother, who, with heat and massage, helped to straighten her legs. By forcing her to walk and continuing treatment for a long time, she was completely cured.

In the old Indian way, Altona was "given away" at the age of thirteen to become the wife of a much older man. It was difficult, with a baby the first year, but she always worked very hard and there was much happiness, too. Her story will be published as part of a series of biographies of outstanding Yukon-Koyukuk area Native people.

Some interesting things happened around Galena, although I didn't stop in the village. There is an Air Force base there, and I was afraid it would be a letdown after Ruby, which really has to be the gem of the Yukon. It was impossible to find a campsite approaching Galena, so I went on by, thinking the Air Force base was on the upriver end of town, as I had spotted some towers and an airfield. That turned out to be the town airport. After getting my camp set up and dinner cooking, my Air Force friends (?) began warming up an F-15—I think it was—just the other side of a bunch of willow trees. Following that a dust storm almost blew me away. By the time I opened my eyes, I almost missed seeing the plane. It flew straight up, gaining speed all the time, and was invisible within less than a minute.

If there had been another such performance, I would have moved, but fortunately there wasn't, and except for a very disagreeable odor, it was a quiet, peaceful night. As I lay in bed thinking about it, I was reminded of the book *The Starship and the Canoe,* by Kenneth Brower. It's the true story of the Freeman family. Father, an astrophysicist, and son, who lives in a tree house, build the ultimate kayak, and consider their home the entire coastline from Vancouver, B.C. to Skagway, Alaska. It reads like a novel. In my case the juxtaposition of the fighter plane with the fish wheel, the technology of the plane and the simplicity of the wheel, continues to make me aware of the difficult position of the Native people.

Down river from Galena, I discovered a perfect example of permafrost, as well as a spot where an ancient wedge had melted out because the river washed away the soil, exposing one side to the light of the sun. The permafrost was still frozen in one place about eight feet below the surface of the ground. The ice wedge left only the triangular hole about six feet across its inverted base, and perhaps twelve feet deep to the apex of the triangle. This ice has been radiocarbon dated in Fairbanks, by objects discovered near the ice wedges found there, to be about 8,500 years old. With thoughts of perhaps finding a tusk protruding from the bank somewhere along the way, I paid close attention and stayed close to the shoreline where the earth was newly exposed. The moss and vegetation make a carpet-like mat over the surface of the soil, and as the earth beneath it washes away, the matting hangs down in shapes closely resembling chocolate drip frosting over the edge of a cake. To add to the fantasy, there are occasional steady drips of water falling from the underside of the matting that glisten and sparkle like a string of diamonds when the sun catches them at just the right angle against the dark, cavernous background.

Now that I've figured a way to lay back against my sleeping bag roll and rest while drifting, I think I could go all night if it were necessary. There have been days of hard paddling against the wind, though, made easier by the sun shining its warmth on my back. One day I did a funny thing because of not having a watch, but I wouldn't have missed it for anything. Just past the village of Koyukuk, where the Koyukuk River flows into the Yukon (in '81 I backpacked along the shore of the north fork of that same river, far away in the Brooks Range), I found a camping place. It had been windy and rainy, so I was tired enough to just fix something to eat and go to bed. After a good many hours of sleep, I heard quite a few boats go by and thought the men were on their way to start their fish wheels. Then I heard planes taking off from Galena, so figured it was time to start the day. So after a good breakfast, I was on the water in an hour. The sky was overcast and temperature cooler, but it wasn't until I had been out an hour that I realized something was wrong.

As I pulled away from shore and the hills and bluffs, I was suddenly aware of seeing lovely sunrise and sunset colors in both east and west directions! I know that in the far north there is a time when the sun travels across the horizon from east to west, always visible, but didn't know that this far north both sunrise and sunset could be seen at one time. It wasn't long before the rising sun took over with awesome colors, and I was left marveling at the wonders of the universe. And laughing at myself thinking that the men returning from their night of partying in town were going to work instead.

Apparently I had gotten up at about 3 a.m., because I arrived in Nulato at 5:30 a.m., at the same time that two seaplanes pulled up to the shore. I hadn't intended to stop, as most villages don't come to life until nearly noon, but the four fishermen who had just flown in from Fairbanks with a guide were insistent that I join them for breakfast at the guide's cabin, which faced the waterfront. No one but a professional could put on a breakfast like that! After they left, I wandered through town, wrote some notes, and finally gave up on seeing anyone else, so left Nulato to its sleep.

# CHAPTER 5

# Unexpected
# Events

# SOLO ON THE YUKON AGAIN

IT SEEMS THAT MY ESTIMATE OF FOUR WEEKS ON THE RIVER WAS CLOSE TO being correct. With about 125 miles to go to St. Mary's, my destination, and about a week to do it in, there should be no problem. Bad storms could make a difference, but hopefully I won't have as much high wind as in the past week. Three layover days in one week were too much. *Layover* is an inappropriate word—*stranded* would be better. On one occasion I was marooned on a wind-swept sandbar island (elevation two or three feet above the river) for most of one day, with rain off and on and only about 100 yards of available walking distance. Needless to say, I finished the book I was reading at the time.

On another day, I was caught late in the evening with no camp-site available and a high wind. So I retreated to the shelter of a cut-bank about twenty feet high, where large trees had fallen into the water, making a natural protection from the wind. I had always thought of the possibility of spending the night in my canoe, and with a waterproof and mosquito-proof sleeping bag cover, it didn't seem like such a bad idea. This was obviously the right time to try it. So, with foam pad in the bottom and the canoe properly tied, it didn't take long for me to be sound asleep, lulled by the rocking motion and sung to sleep by the wind in the poplar trees.

And *then* came the surprise! An odd sound awakened me, and what with the all-night northern daylight, I had no problem seeing that a fairly small black bear was standing on the tree next to me! He was about twelve feet above me, and about the same distance out on the tree trunk, so was looking directly down at me with what appeared to be great curiosity. As I wasn't eager to arouse his anger in any way, I sat up slowly so he could see me, and then proceeded to bang on the sides of the aluminum canoe to see if I could get him to retreat. I was quite sure he wouldn't jump into the canoe, but preferred to see him on the bank, quite naturally.

Eventually (probably 60 seconds), he retreated to the land, so I very quietly got out of the sleeping bag, untied the canoe, and pushed away from the trees. Not satisfied as to who or what I was, he continued to follow me down the bank, at the same rate I was paddling, for 30 or 40 yards before wandering off into the woods.

Later that day I talked to some people at their fish camps and they seem to be having more than the usual amount of trouble with bears in that area. The salmon run is smaller, so there are fewer spawned-out fish for the bears to eat. At the fish camps where the salmon is dried in the open before smoking it, they have dogs to keep away the bears, or at least to warn of their presence.

Diane Calamar, an Alaska Fish and Game employee who is doing a fish count on the river, had just the day before been forced to shoot a bear that had been coming to their tent for food. Incidentally, she proved to me again that all of Alaska is one big small town, as we discovered many mutual friends. Later on downriver, I passed the

*Bear tracks almost everywhere*
*along the river.*

carcass of a dead bear in the river. It wasn't hers, as they were skinning theirs out. And to complete my bear stories, the next night I heard one sniffing and moving around outside my tent. Noise didn't make much impression on the first one, so this time I stayed quiet, and he eventually went away, satisfied, I guess, that I had no food in my tent. All my food stays in waterproof packs in the canoe. I cook away from the tent, and the food is double-wrapped in plastic so that no aroma escapes. I feel pretty safe. Beyond Holy Cross the Natives tell me that there are grizzlies coming into the fish camps. They're something else again, and I try not to camp where I see their tracks.

There has been a change in the type of fishing since earlier on the river. From Kaltag on down, there are fewer and fewer fish wheels and more set nets for dogfish. The dogfish roe is sold to the Japanese as a great delicacy, and as it's against the law to kill the fish only for the eggs, the rest is used for dog food. There is a processing plant for the roe in Kaltag, as well as others closer to the ocean.

There are small mountains on the northwest side of the Yukon just about all the way to St. Mary's, which surprised me. They're not always in view, but they do provide small streams with fresh water, as well as beautiful scenery. There are also large sandbar islands, newly created by the wandering river, that are made up of such a fine sand that any good wind causes real dust storms, similar to those seen on the desert, and complete with the mirage of water rippling, trees elevated from the horizon line, and castles, too, with a bit more imagination. There are fewer birch trees, more willow, and much more evidence of the river choosing its own course. Being closer to the ocean, I'm also closer to the northern tree line, which curves around the coastline of Alaska. The mountains here are all less than 2,000 feet high, but the tree line is at about 1,200 feet, so they are all bald rock domes of varying shapes and sizes.

It's difficult to notice, but there is also a gradual change from Athabascan to Eskimo. From Anvik to Russian Mission the Natives are pretty well mixed. It's interesting that Athabascan is North America's largest native language family, spreading south from Alaska's interior nearly to Puget Sound, then east to the shores of Hudson Bay, and with a large island of Athabascan language speakers in the Southwest, as well as small pockets in California, Oregon, and Washington.

There are interesting place names in all parts of Alaska, and of course the Russian influence is strong throughout much of the state. The town of St. Mary's is on the Andreafsky River, and nearby to Chuckwhoctolik. I passed Yistletaw, but didn't see any evidence of a village. Around the state there are other place names that amused me. Chicken is always the first on the list, as it's rumored that the city fathers in the beginning wanted to name it Ptarmigan, which is the state bird, but couldn't spell it, so said, "To hell with it, let's just call it Chicken." Others are: Purgatory, Lilywig, Burnt Paw, Howling Dog, Deadhorse, Brakes Bottom, Chickaloon, Hungry Village, New Knock Hock, Last Chance, Tin City, Coarse Gold, and Atlasta House.

There is another bit of history related to the Yukon River that I picked up from my USGS topographical maps. For a distance of many hundreds of miles, from southwest of Tanana to Kaltag, there is a dotted line along the northern shore of the river, which is designated "Abandoned telegraph line." It wasn't until I was reading Neil Davis' book *Alaska Science Nuggets* that I realized what it was. It was a part of a pioneer attempt to establish a telegraphic communications link between North America and Europe via the Bering Sea. Cyrus Field's repeated attempts to lay an Atlantic cable ended in failure, giving impetus to an idea originated by Perry Collins. President Lincoln signed an act in 1864 permitting construction to begin the following year. Explorations for the line were divided into three parts: one in British Columbia, where the line from San Francisco terminated, another along the Yukon River and Norton Sound, and the third on the Amur River in Siberia. Little progress was made in Russian America (this was before Alaska was purchased), but by the fall of 1866 the entire route had been surveyed and found suitable.

To save time, it was decided to work through the winter, and it certainly must have been an ordeal for men unaccustomed to such cold and difficult conditions. With only dogs for transportation, and having to thaw the ground before digging in it, it's no wonder that only fifteen miles was completed. But stations were built and thousands of poles were cut and placed along the line. All to no avail, as the Atlantic cable was successfully laid in July of 1866, although the men working in Russian America didn't know it until July 1867. It wasn't all in vain, however, as much worthwhile information about the geography and the flora and fauna of the area was furnished by these men, and it may have played a significant part in the eventual purchase of the territory.

The Native villages continue to surprise me with their friendliness, and I'm often tempted to stay over longer. In Kaltag, the impression was one of busyness, mostly, because they are building sixteen new Native homes, there is a fish roe processing plant there, and the town is obviously in the midst of change. It was a hot, dusty day, and I enjoyed a cold soft drink from a dispenser in the town offices. There are people living in the old landmark church with a tilting steeple on the waterfront, there are tractors in the streets, and bulldozers eating up the earth. And no trees. A hot and hungry dog jumped into my canoe, ate some crackers, and unknown to me, made off with my rain pants. They may find their way home, as I sent back a request, but I've missed them.

The next village downriver was Grayling, which was built only about twenty years ago, so it's a more orderly community. With newer houses, many trees, and the wildflowers in bloom, the appearance of the village is more beautiful than others, but it does lack the timeless quality of the log cabin villages. In Anvik, I stopped only long enough to meet a San Francisco transplant who moved north and is doing a fine job of running the old general store with his Native wife. Near there I met four energetic teenagers who were running a fish camp by themselves, with the aid of about six dogs. Their offer of a cup of coffee was welcome during a rain shower.

In Grayling and Holy Cross the Bureau of Land Management was doing allotment surveys, and I've seen their orange flags tied onto all kinds of rocks and trees along the river. The Native Claims Settlement Act was passed many years ago, but it seems to take a long time to establish all the claims. They work in teams of fifteen or so, set up a camp, and use helicopters for most of their work.

Below Kaltag, I passed what was obviously more than someone's fish camp. There was a cache-style greenhouse, a small tractor, lots of fish drying, and a beautiful new year-around log cabin not far from several older log buildings. The couple invited me in, and I learned that the property has been in the family for three generations, and now that their children are grown, they have retired to live full-time on the river. They are a long way from anywhere, and I enjoyed hearing stories of how they cope.

There is a Cement Hill on the map just before the village of Paradise (which I couldn't find) that is the largest area of exposed conglomerate rock that I've ever seen. Some of the pieces are as big as a car. I passed by Paimiute too early in the morning to stop, but it was a very neat group of five or six cabins which, according to the map, has a population of only one! Maybe all the cabins belong to one person. There was a new flag flying in the small cemetery, so obviously someone cares.

Holy Cross was a pleasant place to visit, and I had an opportunity to get well acquainted with the Walker family who live there. Dave was near the riverbank as I went by thinking about finding a place to camp, and we got to talking. He was building a drying rack for the silver salmon, as the season was about to open, and after I had my tent up I went with him up the hill to his house for water. His wife Lillian invited me for dinner of moose and rice, fresh hot sourdough biscuits with wild raspberry jam, and then after a lot of conversation, suggested that I come for coffee in the morning. Which turned out to be French toast, bacon, grapefruit, and more coffee. They were interesting people. His grandfather was one of the many Russians who married Native women and settled in Alaska in the last century. Good water is a problem in many villages, but the Walkers have an artesian well that flows constantly. They live several miles out of town. A new grandson and his mother were visiting, and I couldn't begin to count the number of other people who came and went while I was there. Reminded me of my own house on occasions.

I said goodbye the next morning, paddled the mile into the town of Holy Cross, went to the post office, and discovered what, to me, was an unusual way to get a message in the Alaskan bush. Zenith is the Alaska Communications Satellite's toll-free telephone service, and knowing that I would be picking up mail in Holy Cross, Celia Hunter had sent a message for me. All I had to do was phone the Zenith operator and ask for message number 33041 (or whatever it was), and it was read to me. All that to change a dinner date in Fairbanks from August 4 to August 5. At about this time I met the Walker's daughter Kathy Chase again. She works for the Tanana Chief's Corporation, so we went to her office for coffee. Then it began to rain, and the longer it rained the less interested I was in getting on the river, so I ended up staying overnight with her and her five-year-old son. And would you believe? I watched my first TV cassette movie, *The Lord of the Rings*—all the conveniences here in the far north. Well, almost all.

Holy Cross has about 250 residents, and even in the rain it impressed me as being a good place to live. At one time there was a Catholic mission and boarding school there, as well as some extensive farming. It was interesting to hear from Dave about the early reindeer herds and the Laplanders who came to teach the Eskimos how to handle them. There are still a few old-time Lapps around, but the experiment failed, as the reindeer bred with the caribou, and now there is only one reindeer herd in Alaska, on Univak Island.

My next communication with anyone was many miles further down the river, when I met two fellows in a rubber raft going back and forth across the river, from a bluff to a sheltered cove and back. They were banding peregrine falcons for Alaska Fish and Game, and were trying to snare one with bait below the nest high on the bluff. Peter Bente, who has formed a corporation, Falco, in Fairbanks, hires himself out just for this work. His assistant is Jorge Albuquerque, from Brazil, who had been studying falcons there, and recently has been enrolled at Brigham Young University in Utah in the zoology department. Peter turns out to be a very good friend of Mary Shields and John Manthei. As a matter of fact, he spent some time last Christmas at their winter cabin, Schimmelpfennig. I hope our paths will cross again. Jorge has invited me to visit his home in Brazil, whether or not he is there.

Russian Mission is a historic location. It was settled by the Russians in the 1700s, and has been continuously occupied since. The population is about 170, and the majority belong to the Russian Orthodox Church, although there is a small Catholic mission here serving five or six families. Being in Russian Mission on the particular Sunday I was proved interesting, as it was the one time in the year that the priests and members of the church paraded all around town, blessing the homes. There are many Russian names here. The first person I met was Pete Petrov, who runs the local store and has lived all his life in this community. Many young children—and dogs of course.

There are indications that the river may be trying to tell me something about when I should be thinking of leaving it. Weather has been more unpredictable, with a lot more wind, and the river has urged me ashore several times. Sometimes gently, occasionally not so gently. I notice, too, that instead of the large, flat-bottom jon-type boats of a hundred miles upriver, all the boats now look like large skiffs designed for use on the rockbound coasts of Maine. So it's good that I'm not trying to go the extra hundred miles to the ocean.

Jan Schofield, my friend from Seldovia, and I are planning to take Wien Airlines special Passport deal that allows 29 days of unlimited flying to all fourteen towns where their jets have regular service. (Plus Seattle, which makes it a great deal, but we can't use that.) It does include St. Mary's, where I end my canoe journey, so Jan is meeting me there and we will tour Alaska by air together for the next month. After that Jan and Ed have invited me to visit them in their new log cabin home outside of Seldovia.

---

Just for fun I've put together my own Murphy's Laws of the Yukon River:

1) No matter in which direction the wind is blowing, it's always coming upriver.
2) What I'm hunting for is always at the bottom of the pack.
3) The best campsites are always found early in the day.
4) A shortcut on the river is always longer; or the fastest current follows the longest route.
5) The bears that I see moving toward me on the sandbars turn out to be stumps 99.9 percent of the time.
6) Just about the time I say ENOUGH (rain, bugs, or whatever), it all changes for the better.

---

Original plans for my canoe trip didn't include going any further down the Yukon River than Holy Cross or Russian Mission at the most. Either of these would mean flying out to a larger nearby town on a mail plane and then transferring once or twice in order to get back to Fairbanks. By going on to St. Mary's, which is another hundred miles or more downriver, I could join Jan Schofield there and arrange to start our tour with Wien Airways. I had no map for this last part of the trip, but the people I talked to in Russian Mission said I would have no trouble—even going upstream on the Andreafsky River where St. Mary's is located.

The day wasn't very auspicious as I paddled away from Russian Mission, to the accompaniment of many children who came to see me off. Being Sunday, the day wouldn't begin for most of the people in town until afternoon, but I was awakened quite early by either a loose dog that looked like a wolf, or more likely, a wolf that looked like a dog, that had disturbed the many chained-up dogs in the village. I was glad to be off before the wind came up on the river.

Below Russian Mission, there is more beautiful country, with bluffs on the right side for a number of miles. The deep colors in the rock are accented by large patches of lichens of brilliant orange, pale green, and several shades of grey. But as much as I enjoy looking at these bluffs, they were beginning to take on a more ominous character as the wind steadily increased after a few hours. At several points where the sheer cliffs rise straight up from the river, there is no place to land, and with the wind blowing very hard against the rock, and the waves approaching a size I no longer wished to deal with, even kneeling in the center of the boat, I began to have my first qualms about further travel downriver unless the weather changed. So as soon as there was a slough that I could sneak into, I landed—in the rain by this time, and put up the tent in a spot that I wouldn't choose under other circumstances. At least it was protected from the wind, and was up from the water, so I tied the canoe and proceeded to settle in, being sure to add extra tie-downs to the tent to keep the rain fly from blowing away.

The rain and wind continued, and at one point during the night I was so concerned about the canoe and the wind that I got up out of

*Unusual rock formation and smaller trees*
*approaching the coast.*

my warm bed, dressed, and fumbled my way through the brush to the shore. The canoe was OK, but the wind was still fierce, so I pulled it all the way up the bank, which was wet, muddy, and slippery, and turned it over to repose in complete safety for the duration.

The duration turned out to be a longer time than I had anticipated. The entire following day was more of the same, except that the rains occasionally let up enough for me to go out and walk around a bit. But the sound of the gales howling around the cliffs and the waves crashing against the rocks made me grateful that I was safely ashore. I slept less well the second night, as I had decided that if the wind stopped at whatever time, I would pack up and leave, in order to get around the hazardous rocks before another wind came up. Sure enough, I awoke suddenly to realize that the trees were no longer swaying and the tent was no longer flapping, and that the strange sensation that had come over me was caused by the lack of noise. I had little conception of time, with no watch, but the nights were not yet dark, so I could see well enough to get everything stowed away and a brief but adequate breakfast eaten, before paddling out onto the barely rippling river. What a relief!

It wasn't long before I paddled off the map and was on my own, grateful for the unusual phenomenon of a tail wind to help me along. The river at this point had changed its course dramatically, and was heading due north for a long straight stretch. After many hours, and only a few decisions to be made about navigation, I came around a bend to discover what looked like a good-sized town on a hillside several miles away. It's always interesting to paddle toward a town from a distance. The buildings that I thought were small dog houses turned out to be homes, and the tiny specks turn into boats and people. It was raining again by the time I arrived and stopped to inquire what town I was in, as well as what time it was. The town was Marshall, and the time only twelve noon. I figured that I had paddled about eight hours, so realized what an early start I must have gotten!

The big general store was closed for lunch, so thinking an orange (or a cup of coffee) would taste good, I inquired about any other place that might be open, and was directed to a very small store in the back room of a house on the main street. When I explained to the very nice Eskimo woman that I had just come off the river, she invited me into her kitchen for coffee, which eventually turned into lunch. A much-appreciated bowl of steaming hot corned beef, barley, and fresh vegetable soup really was just right. The two young daughters were with us, beautifully braided, dressed in their colorful *kuspuks,* and ready to go to a Campfire meeting after lunch.

When her husband joined us, the thought suddenly came to me that it might be wise for me to inquire about a boat ride from Marshall to St. Mary's, as there is no other village between the two. If I were held up again by wind, it could happen that I would miss my connections with Jan and our airline date, so I asked about the possibility of trading my canoe for a trip the seventy miles downriver to St. Mary's. Although there isn't much reason to use canoes on the Yukon, there are many small tributaries that can be navigated by smaller boats and are used for hunting and trapping between fishing seasons. The grandfather in the family had worked on a barge on the river for many years, and wanted to get to St. Mary's, the wife was already busy making up a shopping list, and the husband had, in his mind, already modified a motor mount for a small outboard to fit the canoe.

There was an uneasy feeling in the back of my mind about the last stretch of river, as well as the apprehension concerning time, so, in my usual way, I followed my instincts and gave away my true and faithful canoe, which never leaked a drop in 1,300 miles in two summers on the Yukon. It was a difficult parting, but there was no way I could get it home, and I'm glad that it will be appreciated in the far North. It is now owned by Terry and Gabe Evan of Marshall, Alaska.

The ride to St. Mary's took about two and a half hours, and as we passed one after another separation in the river course and zipped through secret sloughs that were obvious shortcuts to my navigator, I was very happy not to have been making those decisions without a map. Not that I would lose my way, because the braids always come together, but there were great open stretches that we crossed when the waves pounded on the big plywood boat so hard I was afraid it might fall apart. St. Mary's is on the Andreafsky River, which was easy to recognize, as it is a clear river and flows into the Yukon with large swirls of clear, dark brown water. The men unloaded the boat, and helped me carry my gear up the bank to stow under the overhang of the Alaska Commercial Company Store. Still raining.

My only contact in this village was through Mary Shields, who works for Alaska Fish and Game in Fairbanks each summer. She suggested that I call Nancy and James Brady (also Fish and Game), who have lived in St. Mary's for several years. He oversees all the commercial fishing at the mouth of the Yukon, and spends most of the week in and out of Emmonak, a village out on the delta. They have a ten-month-old son, and with James away so much, Nancy was glad to have some company for the week. I had called her earlier from Marshall, so she came to pick me up at the store.

Sorting out (and drying out) my canoeing gear from what belongings I needed to carry in my backpack for the next month and a half didn't take too long. But it did take a rather large box mailed home to pack away for a next trip.

Sometime, I would like to fly low over the mouth of the Yukon River, although merely glancing at a detailed map can give one an idea of how much water there is in the seemingly endless tundra plain. There are three main channels and many smaller ones, meandering through the sedimentary deposit, which is estimated at 100 million tons annually. No wonder anything dropped in the water disappears a few inches below the surface, and rescuing bodies underwater is an utter impossibility. Forty to fifty percent of the delta is wet. It consists of a rough triangle with a base of about fifty miles on the seaward side.

Although treeless and with the horizon a straight line in all directions, there is a profusion of wildlife and small plants that thrive there. It is a haven for migratory birds of many varieties, and, of course, the first step in the salmon's return to its birthplace in the spawning process. This desolate area on the Bering Sea has long been the home of the Yup'ik Eskimos, whose geographic location has made subsistence more difficult than for those further north, who have whales, seals, and caribou to rely on for food and clothing. The early Yup'iks used bird and fish skins for garments and utilized every piece of driftwood that floated down the river, as well as whale bone, for shoring up their mud houses.

There is a comment from a present-day Eskimo that's worth repeating. He said, "In old days, we lived underground and buried our dead above the ground. Now we bury our dead underground and live above ground, and we haven't been warm since." And another phrase that brings out another aspect of the same problem: "We didn't know about being poor until outsiders came and told us we were."

The history of the Yukon River is fascinating, as it has the longest prehistory of any river in this hemisphere, and the shortest history. It is an unglaciated area, and archaeologists have determined that early man crossed the Bering Land Bridge from Asia more than 10,000 years ago—but it wasn't until 1835 that any record of the Yukon River appears, although the Russians had a few settlements along the coast before that time. Trading posts were established at St.

Michael, Russian Mission, and other villages, which became the Russian-American Company, and flourished until the territory was sold to the United States. In 1878, E. W. Nelson (the first non-Russian) arrived in the far North to collect ethnographic material. A portion of this collection is touring Alaska this summer from the Smithsonian Institute, and I had the privilege of seeing it in Juneau.

The Alaska Commercial Company, which has Native-owned stores all over Alaska, was founded in 1869, when a group of Baltimore businessmen bought all the properties of the Russian-American Company, including a fortified post at St. Michael, ships, warehouses, and inventories. The Moravians and the Catholics followed upriver in 1888, with the latter starting a settlement near the mouth of the Yukon and one at Holy Cross. The first was washed away by the river and was rebuilt at Akulerak, about two miles upriver. There the river came close to the mission again, so it was moved in 1950 to its present site at St. Mary's. It has been a boarding school there for many years, and the big three-story, tin-covered buildings stand out sharply against the gentle hillsides of the village.

By 1886, the first of the gold seekers were making their way up the river by sternwheeler, as an alternate route to the Chilkoot Pass from Skagway. This marked the beginning of the industrial era, but it never put an end to the river as provider of food and means of communication for the thousands of Eskimos and Indians along its banks and on its tributaries, which it is today. The ancient burial grounds that remain high above the villages on hills or bluffs are still in use, although for some of the residents are unhappily beginning to slip down the bluffs as spring frost heaves give them a further push. They resemble a miniature city, with tin-roofed spirit houses and white-painted or greyed-out picket fences surrounding them.

St. Mary's has a population of about 450, with two large combination grocery and department stores, a fish-freezing plant, and both public schools and the Catholic mission school. The terrain is certainly different from the previous villages, although similar to Marshall. Rolling tundra hills provide good berry picking. The weather was cooler, but sunny for a change, so we enjoyed being out of doors with the baby. I visited with relatives of the people I met in

Holy Cross, and met many friends of Nancy and Jamie's.

Jan's plane arrived on schedule, and we had several days together in St. Mary's before leaving for Anchorage and the first part of our plane journey to Barrow. As she is writing a guide to wild edible plants in Alaska, she spent a lot of time investigating anything available in the area, and was fortunate to be able to talk with one of the older women in the community on the subject. Her daughter had to translate, as she spoke only her native Yup'ik. Jan was expecting to be tenting with me in St. Mary's, so we laughed a lot about the "hardships" in the bush with hot water, showers, washing machine, and even an electric ice cream machine. One dinner was fresh-caught silver salmon, other goodies, and fresh wild blueberry pies. A fun visit!

# CHAPTER 6

# Farewell River — Hello Arctic

# SOLO ON THE YUKON AGAIN

THE AIRLINES HAVE ROUTED ALMOST ALL PLANES THROUGH ANCHORAGE, SO we had to go there before returning to Fairbanks to say goodbye to my good friends there and pick up my backpack. Saying goodbye involved, among other things, a fine dinner for eleven people the night before we left. Somewhat of a community involvement, but mostly prepared by Celia Hunter and Ginny Wood. Ginny was getting ready to leave for a raft trip, but was not too busy to help with the dinner, which was entirely from their garden and their own chickens. It was a pleasure to have John Manthei's parents, who were visiting John and Mary in Fairbanks, here for dinner also.

The flight to Barrow took less than two hours, and arriving mid-morning, we had a full day before having to locate a sleeping place. Temperature was only 33 degrees when we arrived in this furthest north community in the western hemisphere, where there is no sunset from May 11 to August 5. For three days the town had been fogged in, so it's no wonder the airport was jammed when we arrived! Celia had given us the name of Charlotte Rogers, a public health nurse here, to call, which we did later in the day, as she was working nights. When we reached her, she insisted that we stay in her apartment, which was good news, as the ground everywhere is either mud or wet tundra. Charlotte's apartment closely resembles an Eskimo museum, as she has lived in the North for a number of years and knows many of the local artists who work in ivory, bone, and baleen. Her library is extensive on all Alaskan subjects, so we were glad to be able to spend time with her.

Barrow is an interesting city, with 750 residents, although there are 3,500 in the borough, which is the largest single municipality in the world. Organized in 1972, it has home rule charter—the strongest form of local government allowed under the U.S. constitution. It is entirely above the Arctic Circle, and covers 88.281 square miles. There are eight villages in the borough, and 75 percent are Inupiat Eskimo. Income to the Native Corporation (NANA) was 140 million dollars in property taxes from the oil fields a few years ago.

The atmosphere in Barrow, as a result, is one of activity. There is a housing shortage with so much building going on, and the borough offices alone employ a large number of people. There is a Chinese and a Mexican restaurant, the largest AC store I've ever seen [AC is the largest retailer in rural Alaska], many churches, and more traditionally dressed women. The native language is spoken by almost everyone, though most are bilingual.

Jan and I explored the site of a recent archaeological dig, which last summer exposed the bodies of a family that had been earth-covered and frozen for many hundreds of years. They had been in their home, located near the center of the present town on a small bluff near the shore, when a large ice sheet, or *ivu* [as it is called by the Inupiat] collapsed the roof of their sod house. One body was frozen in such good shape that it was possible to do a complete autopsy on it in Fairbanks. The results are just now being written up. We brought home a few mementos from the excavated area.

The Inupiat language is fascinating to listen to, with its many strong *k* and guttural *g* sounds, but with some words twenty or thirty letters long, it must be difficult to learn. It reflects their needs, as there are 22 different words for snow and snow conditions, and 26

*Whale bones make a fine sign in Barrow.*

different words for ice.

While we were there, we watched men leave to take their boats out around the ice pack, which is only 100 yards off shore, to hunt seals. They still use the traditional *umiak*, made of walrus hide stretched over a wooden frame, as well as wooden outboard boats. Two polar bears have been killed recently because they came into town. Many hides, seal skins, and caribou racks decorate roofs and racks around town. Dogs are not as prevalent here. Probably because the Natives are affluent enough to buy a new snow machine every year.

After two and a half days, we boarded another plane to take us back to Anchorage before our next leg of the journey, to Kotzebue. Watching Barrow recede into the distance from the plane really makes one wonder at how these remarkable people, who had the most complicated technology of all Indians, will meet the challenges of the 21st century.

The flight from Barrow to Kotzebue, both of which are above the Arctic Circle, necessitated another trip in and out of Anchorage. Jan and I are becoming well acquainted with the airport, which truly is international in flavor, but we've never had much time to spend there. Fortunately, friends of friends and relatives of friends have provided room for us when we have had to stay overnight. The only problem is that we won't be able to visit all of the people in Anchorage whose names have been given to us. Perhaps another time.

On my last trip to Alaska, I spent a few days camping in Kotze-bue, so Jan and I returned to the same spot on the beach. We set up our tent not far from the dozen or so familiar-looking traditional white canvas tents of the Native fish camps, and set out to learn what we could of the area.

Kotzebue is twenty-six miles above the Arctic Circle on Alaska's Northwest Coast. The nearby Kobuk, Noatak, and Selwick River deltas helped to establish the site as an early center of arctic commerce. An active trade in furs, skins, and tools supported a flourishing village known as Kikiktagruk when Captain Otto von Kotzebue came upon it in 1816. The city is now the center of activity for 3,000 people and is the headquarters for NANA, one of the twelve Native regional corporations in the state.

Eleven million acres of the region are now parts of the Cape Krusenstern, Kobuck Valley, Gates of the Arctic, Noatak, and Bering Land Bridge National Monuments. Some of North America's most ancient cultures have been discovered at Cape Krusenstern, where beach ridges added over 9,000 years are yielding a record of continuous habitation. The Noatak National Preserve is the largest undisturbed mountain-ringed watershed in North America, and is a U.S. Biosphere Reserve. The Kobuk Valley National Park is over a million acres, preserved for environmental, archeological, and subsistence values, and includes the Kobuk Sand Dunes and Onion Portage. The Bering Land Bridge was a thousand-mile-wide corridor that connected Alaska and Siberia during the Ice Ages. This two-and-a-half-million-acre monument has archeological sites, thermal activity, and important wildlife habitat.

Over 80 per cent of the population is Inupiat Eskimo, who continue to pursue traditional lifestyles with some modifications. Jan and I watched the men putting out their gill nets just offshore for the harvest of silver, or cohoe, salmon, and watched as they brought in their catches to be weighed and paid for. There are a few processors in Kotzebue, but most fish are shipped out fresh by air. Until the Marine Animal Protection Act of 1973, Kotzebue was known as the polar bear hunting capital of the world. Now the animals are only killed if they endanger the lives of inhabitants.

Reindeer herding has been revived some in recent years. It was introduced before 1910, but due to interbreeding with the caribou and overgrazing, the herds have decreased in size. Nearby Jade Mountain is the source of a hard jade that has been cut, polished, and traded by local Inupiat for at least 700 years, and is available in local stores.

There is considerably more vegetation around Kotzebue than we saw in Barrow, and Jan was able to find several new varieties to add to her collection of edible wild plants. We were impressed with a vegetable-growing project sponsored by the Native Corporation, and saw a number of local gardens that seemed to be thriving in their plastic dome environments.

In spite of two days of rain, our visit to Kotzebue was a good one.

*Eskimo woman picking blueberries.*
*Note the* mukluks.

It is a friendly town, and because of the weather, we spent more time indoors than usual, so became well acquainted with the local Dairy Queen (believe it or not!) and the large Native-owned hotel, which served excellent meals.

The flight from Kotzebue to Nome was the only direct one we've had. All others have had to return to Anchorage in between, but this trip took only 40 minutes to reach the Southwest Coast of the Seward Peninsula, where Nome is located. It was around supper time when we came across the low coastal mountains and glided into the airport, a few miles out of town. Our plans to stay at the local youth hostel were blocked when we discovered that it had closed at the end of the previous summer. A young couple from the plane shared our dilemma, so we pooled our resources and rented a room at the "cheap" hotel, which didn't turn out to be such a great idea. Too much partying going on all night up and down the halls.

Before we decided to set up our tent on the windy beach, we called a friend of Charlotte Rogers' (the nurse we stayed with in Barrow), who owns the nicest gift shop in Nome. She was most friendly, and suggested her floor or couch would be more comfortable then the beach. Finding no reason to disagree with her, we accepted her invitation with great pleasure.

There are close to 3,500 people living in Nome, and about 65 percent are Eskimo. It is an industrial and educational center for a much larger area, however, and has a new community college, as well as a hospital and a variety of stores. Air tours fly to Nome, so there are the usual tourist-oriented aspects of the town, too. Our hostess, Mary Knodel, has one of the finest collections of ivory carvings in the North in her store, along with every other Eskimo craft, including a $12,000 polar bear coat with hood, which should undoubtedly be in a museum. This was my summer not to buy, but it was a great temptation—not the coat, only a few carvings!

Beach combing is a fun thing to do in Nome, and it calls to mind the pictures taken in 1900, when gold was discovered on the beach and 20,000 people set up tents in the area. There are still companies dredging for gold near Nome, and Jan and I enjoyed talking with two fellows who had a small sluicing operation going on the beach. Jan even tried her hand at gold panning and did fairly well for so short a time. We also spent time talking with a very enthusiastic Eskimo woman who is a local authority on edible wild plants. It was fortunate that Jan had a tape recorder because she talked too fast for anyone to take notes.

The flight back to Anchorage from Nome took us, as usual, over spectacular snow-covered mountain ranges with amazing views of great ice fields and glaciers. We have been fortunate to have most of our flights on clear days, so we have often seen Mount McKinley from as far as 150 miles away. One day, flying above the clouds, we were

*There are thousands of square miles of
uninhabitable tundra in Alaska.*

impressed with the sight of McKinley and Foraker peaks appearing
above the clouds, bathed in the rosy glow of a setting sun. There are
thousands of square miles of tundra to see, too, and until a person
has flown over Alaska, there is no way of realizing how much water is
a part of the land. Flying is also the only way to see the tremendous
distances between settlements, and how much of it is uninhabitable,
although many tiny villages dot the river systems around the state. It
was a thrill to see the volcanoes Illiamna, Redoubt, Augustine, and
Spur on our way from Dillingham. All are classified as active,
although there have been no eruptions for a number of years.

CHAPTER 7

# Southwest
# Adventures

DILLINGHAM, OUR NEXT TOWN TO VISIT, IS ON THE SOUTHWEST COAST OF Alaska, and is in a part of the state unfamiliar to me. It is located on Bristol Bay at the confluence of the Wood and Nashagak Rivers, and is the area's major population center. With no contacts there, Jan and I made some inquiries and found that the best place to camp was adjacent to the harbor, complete with shower facilities. As it turned out, the harbor was being dredged by the Army Corps of Engineers at whatever time the tides allowed, so we were lulled to sleep and awakened by the sound of the dredge. But the tent was located in the midst of a huge patch of mastodon plants (so named because a mastodon was unearthed some years ago that had the remnants of some of these plants in its stomach), and in spite of rain and a large number of black flies, we enjoyed our visit there. The rain made the pleasant new library/museum an even more attractive place to us, along with the fine new hotel restaurant. One evening we joined the townspeople in their weekly bingo game, held at the volunteer firemen's hall. It was our first exposure to "serious" bingo. Interesting.

Jan had a friend in the neighboring village of Manokotak, so we arranged for the fifteen-minute flight there from Dillingham for an overnight stay with the Crace family. Marilyn teaches there and her husband Tim is a pilot, carpenter, guide, oil-well driller, skin sewer, cook, poet, playwright, and journalist. It helps to be versatile if you want to make it in Alaska. Their two very bright children added to the pleasure of our visit. Manokotak is a small Native village and is unique in the state, as the residents themselves have paid for their own improvements, housing, and even their own satellite tele-communications system. With all the federal and state funds available for the villages, this is an almost unheard-of situation. The residents of Manokotak are to be commended.

It was obvious when we arrived that this was a "different" community. Their two big cleanup days a year have reduced the usual clutter that we see in most villages, and to arrive at 10 a.m. and find everyone up and busy is quite unusual. These Eskimos are proud of their community and work hard to maintain it. Average income per family is $40,000, according to Marilyn, which is very high for a village. The Bristol Bay area is one of the world's largest fisheries, and they have had a good season this year, as opposed to the salmon runs on some of the rivers.

There are fine craftsmen and women in the area, too, and I'm constantly amazed at how many artists and skin sewers there are among both the Natives and the whites, and both men and women. I've see lynx hats, sealskin slippers and mukluks, cuffed fur mitts, and beautifully crafted clothing of fur that is incredibly designed and sewn. Most of it is not for sale. The Craces have an outstanding collection of Eskimo yo-yos that make me wish I could add to mine.

The general area around Manokotak is flat, wet tundra terrain, accented with small lakes and meandering rivers that almost meet themselves on each hairpin turn toward the sea. There are low mountains (high hills?) in the distance, and one that is a backdrop for a real bird's-eye view of the country.

The Cessna 206 that returned us to Dillingham was full, with six Native women and a few children, all chattering in their own dialect. We learned that time is never a fixed point in their lives, as departure for the plane was scheduled for "between 9:00 and 10:00," so of course it was 10:00 by the time we got off the ground.

The following is a poem that was written by a school girl from Dillingham, and it gives such a good picture of a visit to a fish camp that I thought I'd share it with you.

## LEWIS POINT BY VICKIE DULL

I visited fish camp last summer.
My cousins invited me up to eat.
We passed little shacks
With their doors open to let in an elusive breeze.
Kids ran by
Saying hi and asking about friends at home.
We passed fish racks and smoke houses.
Full with king and red salmon.
Women and girls
Were splitting the day's catch
And adding them to what was already on the racks.

SOLO ON THE YUKON AGAIN

We entered the canvas tent.
It was cool inside after the heat of outdoors.
I was given a bowl of hot fish soup
That had been cooked over a Coleman stove.
The soup was so good
I had thirds.
After eating
We walked to the river bank
And watched the tide go out.
Kids gathered and started a game of volleyball.
A fish net hung between two poles on the tundra
And a child's plastic ball.
We played until the sun went down.
Back in the tent with the kerosene lamp burning
We drank tea and talked about the changing weather.
Bedtime we crawled into our sleeping bags.
I lay there and watched black spiders
Scurry across the sides of the tent
Hoping they wouldn't decide to sleep with me.
Morning came and coffee was boiling.
We washed our faces in a little basin.
After breakfast we walked through fish camp.
From every shack,
"Come and have coffee."
Soon it was time to go.
I didn't want to leave.

A few hours in Dillingham, a short flight to Anchorage, a few hours there, and by early evening we were in McGrath. The Anchorage layover was just long enough to have supper and spend an exciting hour waiting for a small Cessna to make an emergency landing because it had lost a wheel. The fire engines had foamed the runway, emergency vehicles were all over the place, lights were flashing, and hundreds of people were watching for the moment of set down. With only one wheel plus a tail wheel, any slight bump could send the small plane into a flip, so it was with one great yell of joy that we watched the pilot bring down the plane without a mishap and slide in on the foam. There have been several fatal accidents in small planes lately, but considering that there are more private planes here than in any other city, the statistic isn't so surprising.

McGrath is on the Kuskokwim River, about halfway between Fairbanks and Bethel, on the coast. Among other things it is a stop on the Iditarod Race trail, and is a central hub for a large area. There is a Federal Aviation Authority flight station there, and a National Weather Bureau station as well. The population is about 450, divided half and half between Native and white. In appearance it is more well-kept than most towns, with many houses having yards of grass as well as flowers. Almost unheard of in the smaller communities. The main street faces the airplane runway and the runway borders the river. These are the only two means of access except dog team, and as the Iditarod Race is such a big event, there are a number of dog teams in and around town.

It was a surprise to be met at the plane by Gordon Castanza and Beverly Cornet, whom I had met when I was in Skagway the first of June. I had tried to reach him by phone without success, but had called someone else whose name had been given to me earlier, and she had called Gordon. So rather than tenting, we enjoyed their hospitality for a three-day visit. Gordon ran the Iditarod Race in 1980, and was the third person entered for next year's race, which takes place in March. It was interesting to hear his stories about the race and to see his dogs.

Our days were full of any number of activities. Jan and I always try to do something that will more or less repay our friends for their kindness, and this time we almost overdid ourselves. Besides helping clean out and scrape a good-sized skiff to ready it for painting, we offered to help Gordon clean out his septic tank. In this village, that means renting a pump and a portable tank and doing the job yourself, and as in most amateur situations, there are always things that go wrong. It was an experience I wouldn't care to repeat, but guess I can chalk it up to experience. Dinner at the local roadhouse was fun. The owner is an elderly New England-type woman, whose true personality only comes through when she speaks. She is a tough, crusty old woman who orders her guests around as if they were hired help, refuses to serve anyone if they arrive ten minutes late, and serves family style for only twelve at a time. She even dictates what a person can't have—for example, I couldn't have ice cream on my pecan pie. Just as well.

Another visit in Anchorage between planes brought Jan and me back to Jana Thalacker's home before leaving the next morning for King Salmon and Katmai National Park.

As head of an airline parts department, it was easy for Jana to get us to the plane in plenty of time to stand in line the necessary half hour or more that was needed to check baggage through. No chore to wait, however, as people watching is certainly more interesting there than anywhere else I know. There were people with enough baggage to set up a whole tent city. Probably hunting parties with guides. There were people with boxes and boxes of frozen fish, and I wished for some myself. One hundred-pound halibut would only cost about thirty dollars excess baggage to ship, but that's only the beginning of the cost. At any time we could glance around and see thirty or forty coolers containing either fresh or frozen fish, securely tied and sealed, waiting to be checked in. There were people dressed like New York City next in line to some who looked as if they had spent the summer in the bush with neither soap nor water. Great contrasts.

In our preplanning, Jan and I had arranged to visit Katmai National Park toward the end of our trip, because, after reading and studying about the area, it seemed that this could well be the high spot of the trip. To get to Katmai, which is almost 400 miles southwest of Anchorage, it's necessary to fly to the town of King Salmon and transfer there to a small amphibian plane for the short flight over the lakes and mountains to Naknek Lake, where Brooks Lodge and the Park Service campground is located. The area around the Lodge is well known as a world class fishing area, with rainbow trout, lake trout, Dolly Varden trout, and grayling, silver, and sockeye salmon found in the Naknek River system.

After the rather barren, treeless area around King Salmon, we were surprised to see so many glacial lakes and dense spruce forests, which change to tundra as the elevation increases. The campground

*Jan and some good-sized moose horns in
Katmai National Park.*

has about twenty tent sites, a number of shelters with tables, and the absolutely necessary caches for storing all food out of reach of the great brown bear, whose home this area has always been. To clear up any questions, the brown bear is the same animal as the grizzly, but in the coastal areas and on the islands they are known as brown bears, whereas in the interior they are called grizzlies. The brown bear grows larger because he has an easier life and a better diet, due to his geographic location. Brown bears usually weigh between 500 pounds and 1,000 pounds, although larger ones are occasionally seen.

These magnificent creatures are, at this point in time, sharing their fishing grounds with a limited number of people at a time who come to visit the park, but only because the Park Service has been very careful to instruct everyone as to the inherent dangers involved in a possible conflict between man and bear. After the rangers acquainted us with our environment, we were free to pursue our own desires, which included taking advantage of each day's guided nature walk and each evening's presentation by a member of the staff. There are many short trails around the camp, all originally made by the bears, so it pays to be very alert and to make enough noise to let them know you're coming. They are unpredictable, but normally don't want to interfere unless you threaten them in some way. So we tied a jingle bell on Jan's shoe and covered the area pretty well.

*Much too close! Jan took this picture*
*of a foolish photographer.*

There is an Eskimo dwelling that has been restored by the Park Service, which was an interesting thing to see. Called a *barabara* (accent on the second syllable), it is one of twenty or thirty in the area, but is the only one that has been restored. These are underground, sod-covered houses that were used by the Aleuts and Eskimos up until the time the white man changed their way of life.

Back to the bears: The second day we saw a mother and one cub swimming in the river for a long time. She was being lazy and was fishing for spawned-out salmon that were still edible. At one point, she caught one, took it to the bushes, and although we couldn't see her, the baby bear set up a terrible howl—apparently mother wasn't being generous enough with her meal. By the end of the next day, we

*The great brown bears walk the shores near*
*the campground every day.*

stopped counting how many bears we had seen. Bears catching silver salmon in the falls, bears walking along the beach bordering our campground only thirty feet away, and bears blocking the bridge over the river by lying down to feed on a large salmon in the bushes next to the bridge. When this happens, the rangers come and shoot delayed-action firecrackers at the animal in order to make him move. It seems to work. They had to do the same thing when a careless camper left a bag of granola on the table at our campsite. The bear came at 5:30 a.m. and took it, then returned the next morning at 5:35 to discover a ranger there with the scare-gun. A few days of that and it seemed to reprogram the bear's actions, but it points out the fact that if the people and the bears are to get along, everyone must be very careful. They are magnificent creatures, and I spent a lot of time with my eyes glued to my field glasses in order to see them close up.

Katmai is probably best known for being the location of the Valley of Ten Thousand Smokes, where in 1912 forty square miles of lush green land was buried under volcanic deposits as much as 700 feet deep. Severe earthquakes had rocked the area for a week before Novarupta Volcano exploded. The force was so great that the air was filled with ash, pumice, and gas, which darkened the atmosphere over most of the Northern Hemisphere. Fortunately, the warning quakes alerted the people living in the area, and the accounts of their reactions and escape are interesting to read. The area remained deserted until 1915, when Dr. Robert Griggs of the National Geographic Society explored it, and named it the Valley of Ten Thousand Smokes because of the many steaming fumaroles. There are only a few fissures where steam is escaping at the present time. Since the eruption, the Ukak River and its tributaries have cut deep, narrow gorges through the ash deposits, and life is slowly returning to the valley.

One day we joined a group to take the drive to the valley, accompanied by park personnel. The forty-mile drive over a very primitive road included three stream crossings which would be pretty scary in high water. There is a Park Service cabin at the end of the road and a trail down to the river bed and the valley, rather resembling a mini Grand Canyon. There is potential for new eruptions in this part

*The Ukak River has cut canyons through 70-foot walls of compacted volcanic ash in the Valley of Ten Thousand Smokes.*

of the state, as plumes of smoke arise from several surrounding mountains, and Mount Trident has erupted four times in the last two decades, the most recent being in 1969. It was a beautiful walk down into the canyon. We had plenty of time to take pictures, rest, and just soak up the atmosphere—and the weather cooperated.

The pumice rocks which cover the area are fascinating. They come in all sizes, shapes, and colors along the lakeshore. They float in water. A bushel basket filled would only weigh a few pounds. And most surprising, when a person walks on the smaller rocks on the beach, they actually feel soft underfoot.

We met a number of interesting people who shared our campsite. Some were planning to spend a week or two backpacking in the park. Some were professional wildlife photographers, and some were there only for the fishing, but most people came to appreciate, as we did, the wildness of this remote park and the opportunity to visit the brown bear on his own terms.

Then on to our last plane trip of this month-long excursion: back to Anchorage and, with only a short wait between planes, on to Kodiak Island for a few days. I had spent almost a week in Kodiak in 1981, and because my memories were so good, was glad to be returning with Jan. The entire town was rebuilt following the '64 earthquake, and is now an attractive small city stretching up the sides of the nearby low-lying mountains, and surrounding the large boat harbor. It was the first Russian settlement in America, and is one of the nation's top fishing ports, although recently the king crab industry has been unsuccessful. The U.S. Fish and Wildlife Service manages almost 2,000 acres of National Wildlife Refuge on the island, which can be reached only by boat or float plane. There are eleven cabins available free for hunting and fishing, but reservations must be made early for the drawings, which are held four times a year.

An interesting thing happened to us when we arrived in Kodiak. When we were in Nome, we met a young man from Kodiak who suggested that we might like to stay at his house. "Plenty of room on the floor," he said. "The door is always open." So armed with his kind invitation and directions, we took a cab in from the airport to his

*The Russian Orthodox church in Kodiak.*

house. The building is three stories, two apartments, and was in the process of being remodeled. The ideal location, overlooking the harbor, is convenient to everything. Sure enough, the door was open, so we dropped our packs behind a chair and went out to see the town. It was about noon then. When we returned about supper time, we found the door locked and no one home, so we went out for dinner. Then returning to find nothing changed, we explained our plight to the girls downstairs, who took us in for the evening. They reassured us that Bob Brodie really did live upstairs, but couldn't tell us where he was. After several hours, they suggested that we try to get in from the balcony just above their front door. This was accomplished by one girl getting up on a chair, then standing up on my shoulders and hoisting herself onto the balcony. Success! So about the time we were ready for bed, a fellow came in who was renting a room from Bob. He hadn't seen our packs and had locked the door when he went out. Bob returned from Anchorage the next day. We had a huge halibut dinner for assorted friends and a lot of good conversation, too, so our visit was an excellent one.

There are a number of smaller islands surrounding Kodiak. One just opposite the city has recently been made accessible because an addition to the harbor has been built there, and a six-passenger ferry runs back and forth all day and half the night. There is a bridge to the island under construction, which could spoil it as a wildlife and nature sanctuary. Jan and I spent a day on it, hiked its two-mile length, browsed around looking for plants, eating the last of the salmonberries and enjoying the peace and quiet. The only occupants of the island are three small ponies who have made trails over and around and through the dense alder tree and Sitka spruce forest. The only problem was that the ponies are only about four feet tall, so their well-worn trails kept us in some strange positions. The tide was out, so we examined beached jellyfish, collected shells, and in general enlarged my knowledge of saltwater plants. Did you know the bull kelp is the fastest growing plant in the world? And that it reaches a length of two hundred feet in some parts of the ocean? And that pickled bull kelp is a real treat to eat?

The *Cry of the Wild Ram* is a historical pageant put on every year during the third week in August. It is a fine portrayal of Alexander Baranof, who governed the Russian-American colony for nearly thirty years, from 1790 to 1819, and an excellent reenactment of those years. I was sorry we were just too late to see it.

Leaving Kodiak by Alaska ferry for the overnight trip back to

Homer reminded me of my long trip out the Aleutian Chain in '81 aboard the same ship—the *Trusty Tusty*, whose full name is the M/V *Tustumena*. Sleeping bags kept us comfortable, as there is a touch of fall in the weather by the first of September. Jan's husband Ed had been working in Homer, so it was a happy reunion at the ferry dock when he met us after our month-long flying trip.

Ed Berg's daughter and friend had returned to Madison, Wisconsin, so he was free to join us at the Schofield's for a week, along with a charming German couple whom Jan and Ed met in Homer.

We chartered a small boat (a friend of Ed Berg's) to take us the several hours' trip across Kachemak Bay to the closest landing place to the cabin, which is Jackalof Bay—still seven miles from their house. With a load of supplies as well as our packs, the Toyota Land Cruiser made two trips over the partially washed-out road, and we all breathed a sigh of relief when we arrived safely at Jan and Ed's cabin.

I knew that in the two years between 1981, when I visited them in a cabin they were renting outside of Homer, and this summer, they had completed a 14-foot by 20-foot log cabin. Actually, they did the construction during the summer of '82, and moved in September. But I wasn't prepared for what a beautiful place it was—both the country and the cabin. These are the foothills of the snow-covered mountains we see from across the bay, and the Schofield's cabin nestles in a small meadow surrounded by large Sitka spruce. The Rocky River, a few hundred feet below the house, brings ice-cold, crystal-clear water tumbling over the boulders to them. An unpredictable river, it washed out a bridge and destroyed the road the day they moved in. Only temporary repairs were done, as it is an abandoned logging road, and can only be used a part of the year. It's seventeen miles to the village of Seldovia, where the ferry docks, but only miles to a small boat harbor. So any way you look at it, life isn't easy, but it has its own special rewards.

In the winter time, access is by skis, so Jan and Ed have trained Maxwell, their Doberman, to pull a sled while they ski with packs. Maxwell's other mission in life is to change people's negative feelings about the breed. He is so gentle that he seems to apologize if he bumps into you.

*Jan and Ed's new cabin on Swift Creek.*

The cabin is one of the most attractive that I've seen. With herbs growing in window boxes, homemade furniture, plenty of cupboards, and a spacious loft, it gives a feeling of warmth and hospitality sometimes lacking in bush cabins. We managed six people for five days with no problems. It's hard to believe that the two of them did the construction alone, with only the aid of a come-along.

*Ed Berg joins the Schofields at their modern, up-to-date post office.*

An interesting note: The Schofield's mailing address is Red Mountain, via Homer, Alaska. Their post office is a ten-foot square tarpaper-covered shack on the beach, up on pilings to accommodate the tides. The pilot of the mail plane drops the mail inside the door a few days a week, weather permitting. It's then sorted into the residents' cardboard boxes, gallon jugs, laundry bags, or whatever container they choose, by the first one who comes for the mail. I would guess that about fifteen people share this service.

It was great fun to explore the area, hiking through the dense forests or scrambling along the rocky beach. Ed Berg is teaching a geology class in Homer, and plans to bring a field trip over to check out a number of interesting features of the land, so between that and Jan's edible plant interest, I feel as if I were a student again. Indelible memories include: a fifty-foot waterfall part way up a mountain, bushwhacking through the hazardous devil's club, thorns among moss-covered trees, sitting quietly beside a clear fishing pool in the river watching the trout and the salmon, sharing a birthday party with our special friends from Germany, and finally, packing all six of us, four backpacks, and Maxwell-dog into a Toyota Land Rover to make the hazardous trip back to the town of Seldovia, and the ferry to Homer.

Three days in Homer at Ed Berg's house gave me time to say goodbye to my friends there, pack up another box to mail home, and get ready to hitchhike to Glenallen to meet Carl Bauers, who was planning to leave for Woodruff, Wisconsin within the following week. So, hoping to take advantage of weekend traffic heading home to Anchorage on Sunday, I was out on the road by late morning. After about half an hour of turning down shorter rides, a man came along with a truck full of wood and a lot of miscellaneous things, who said he was going to Anchorage. So again I was fortunate. By late afternoon, we arrived in the big city, and I tried, successfully at last, to reach a couple who are good friends of my best friends, whom I had tried to find at home off and on during both of my Alaskan trips. They immediately dropped everything and drove across the city to pick me up, in spite of my protestations that there is a bus, and I spent several beautiful days with Jack and Lyn Peterson. They live in a very nice ground-floor condominium, only a few blocks from downtown and two blocks to the water. Great fun. Even managed to go to the theater one evening.

Hitchhiking out of Anchorage is fairly easy, as the bus service extends well out of town to include neighboring settlements. It was about a forty-five minute wait, but eventually a big new pickup pulled up with a man who was going home to Valdez and could easily drop me off in Glenallen. It was a beautiful drive through the mountains, and I was glad to arrive there by mid afternoon.

I guess Carl Bauers was glad to see me, too. He had broken his leg sometime previously in a logging accident, the cast had just been removed a few days before, the leg was weak, and the ankle still sore, so he was very much on crutches. The following day was spent pleasantly, having lunch with the Senior Citizens, meeting friends, and generally getting ready to leave. That included turning off the water, as Carl didn't plan to return until spring, which was the biggest job. On the trip home, it took me a little while to get accustomed to such a large truck after driving my small one, and the power steering took a little adjustment on my part to get used to. With great patience, Carl put up with my driving for the entire trip. We were fortunate to have mostly good weather and good driving conditions on the Alaska Highway, with the exception of one stretch in the Yukon mountains, in a blizzard at night, with many trucks on the road. That didn't last too long, and we eventually found a place where we could get off the road and sleep in the truck.

So, five days and 3,000 miles later, we pulled into the Bauers' driveway in a pouring rain. I called my son and daughter-in-law, Dare and Mary, and began the slow process of adjustment to life in northern Wisconsin again.

Certainly there is a lifetime full of memories of these two summers' Alaskan trips that bring me warm feelings and joyous moments to recall, and the most heartwarming have to be the friendships that I've made in so many different and varied places around the state. I'm very sure that in the next few years I will return to spend more time with these people ... time that just wasn't enough on this last trip. Then sometime, just perhaps, I may be willing to settle down in my one-room cabin on the river.

IN CLOSING, I'D LIKE TO LEAVE YOU WITH THIS QUOTE FROM BOB WEEDEN, A well-known writer from Fairbanks:

"The world needs an embodiment of the frontier mythology, the sense of horizons unexplored, the mystery of uninhabited miles. It needs a place where wolves stalk—because a land that can produce a wolf is a healthy, robust, and perfect land. The world desperately needs a place to stand under a bright auroral curtain on a winter's evening, in awe of the cosmic cold and silence. But more than these things, the world needs to know that there is a place where men live amidst a balanced interplay of the goods of technology and the fruits of Nature. Unless we can prove that a modern society can thrive in harmony with the land, the bits of wilderness we salvage in Alaska will be nothing more than curious artifacts in the sad museum of mankind."

CPSIA information can be obtained at www.ICGtesting.com
Printed in the USA
LVOW07s2144170815

450451LV00002B/461/P